Hopkins Educational

SAT®
PREP
2021

Contents

About this Book 1

How to use this book... 2

Exam Secrets! 3

Preparing for exams 4

About the SAT 7

Strategies 17

SAT English Writing and Language... 34

SAT Math 53

SAT Reading 77

SAT Essay Prompt 95

Practice Test.. 116

    Section 1: SAT Reading... 116

    Section 2: SAT Writing and Language... 144

    Section 3: SAT Math No Calculator.. 159

    Section 4: SAT Math Calculator 166

    Section 5: SAT Essay Prompt.. 178

Answers 181

    Section 1: SAT Reading... 181

    Section 2: SAT Writing and Language... 198

    Section 3: SAT Math No Calculator.. 206

    Section 4: SAT Math Calculator 210

    Section 5: SAT Essay Prompt.. 223

Scoring Guide.. 230

About this Book

This book is a no-nonsense guide to acing your SAT. I will teach you about the different question types, how to study, how to prepare on the day, how to ace the exam on the day and get into the school of your dreams. Crucially, I will tell you all the secrets of the SAT exam that will help you to find shortcuts, answer questions quickly, and completely comprehend the nuances of the SAT.

A lot of books have excess detail and boring content, but not this one! I have cut the fluff and made a fast-paced guide ready to help you get the most out of every second. I have included all the key details you need to give you the key ingredients to acing your SAT.

I will not only teach you how to master each question type, but I will also show you how to maximize your efforts; both in studying, and in the exam room! So many students have the knowledge but underperform on the day, with my hints and tips you will get every point available to you for your knowledge.

It is best used as a study guide, read it, get the information that you need, and then study each section of questions independently. Use my useful hints and tips on effective studying (proven by research) and then, when you're ready, attempt the practicetests.

I wish you the best of luck in your studies, and hope that this book gets you into the school that you desire!

How to use this book

You can't underestimate the importance of doing well in the high-pressure high-stakes environment of test day. How well you do on the SAT will have a significant impact on your future- and I have the research and practical advice to help you execute on test day.

The book you're reading now is designed to help you avoid the most common errors test-takers frequently make.

It will show you tricks, tips and hints to answering the exam, not only having the bank of knowledge required but also managing the exam situation to your advantage, which questions to target and how to maximize your marks. It is crucial that you study this part of the book as closely as the content. It is these techniques that will change a good score into an excellent score!

I suggest going through it a number of times, as repetition is an important part of learning new information and concepts.

First, read through the study guide completely to get a feel for the content and organization. Read the general success strategies first, and then proceed to the content sections. Each tip has been carefully selected for its effectiveness.

Second, read through the study guide again, and take notes highlighting those sections where you may have a particular weakness.

Finally, take the practice test and use it to see where you need to improve, then return to those areas.

Finally, bring the Study guide with you on test day and study it before the exam begins.

Exam Secrets!

This section is all about how best to prepare for any exam, before and after, it's worth reading: get all the details you need about preparing and how to SAT in an exam!

With any and all exams it is absolutely crucial that you prepare properly and that you have all the hints and tricks that you can have, available to you. The whole point of this book is to help you, not only learn about the SAT, about each question type and to practice the exams but also to help you get every extra mark that you can.

No time to hang about; let's look at how best to prepare for tests and exams.

Preparing for exams

I spoke to the experts and have all the details on how to prepare for exams (of any kind!). You should treat the SAT like any other normal exam and prepare for it in the ways that your teachers would have wanted you to prepare in high school! Prepare effectively in the build-up to it and you will get the score that you need. If you follow this advice you give yourself the best chance of acing your SAT, and any other exam for that matter so, as I teach you all about the rest of the exam, make sure you follow the good study habits all the way!

Without further ado, please check out my advice below.

Good Study Habits - what to do in the build-up to the exams.

1. Don't cram at the last second; try studying for 60-90 minutes per day for a week leading up to an exam. All-nighters simply don't work for most people, and students experience declining returns on their efforts when they attempt to study for four and five hours straight.

2. If you have any outstanding questions, go and get help at least three days before. You'll be able to go see somebody with an agenda if you've given yourself a mock test in advance.

3. Think about what written questions on the exam might be; outline potential essays as a form of pre-testing and practice.

4. Use the elimination process on multiple-choice questions. Cover the options first for multiple choice questions, and try answering the question on your own. Thus, you will find the options for the answer less confusing. Make sure that you are aware of context, relationships and positionality between concepts, and multiple definitions of terms, as you prepare for multiple choice exams. A deep understanding of the vocabulary is a key to multiple-choice exam success.

5. Keep up with your work. If you attend class regularly, keep up with reading, and take notes conscientiously, studying can be a relatively pain-free process. Make sure to review and expand upon class notes regularly throughout the semester. Consider developing a

glossary or collection of note cards for vocabulary review in each class. Many students find that preparing for an individual class for 60-90 minutes per day, five or six days per week, will leave them well-prepared at exam time.

6. Find a group of other committed students to train with. A group study session is an ideal time for reviewing and comparing notes, asking each other questions, explaining ideas to each other, discussing the upcoming examination and difficult concepts, and delegating study tasks where appropriate. Set your group study session with an agenda and a specific timeframe, so that your work together is not off-topic.

7. Make sure you get lots of sleep. The time spent asleep is often the time when we synthesize information completely, especially the topics that are covered in the few hours before bedtime. Once you take the test you want to be as new as possible to be able to fully engage your working memory.

8. Find ways to apply class materials. Think about how course topics relate to your personal interests, societal issues and controversies, issues that have been raised in other classes, or different life experiences.

9. Develop a good routine 'morning-of' Eat a good breakfast. Go ahead and play something upbeat if the music gets you going. Get some physical exercise, even if it's a brief walk or stretch. If you feel nervous, record your anxieties on paper or use mental imagery to imagine doing something you enjoy and then apply those feelings to the exam. Think of preparing for a performance like an athlete before a contest or a musician.

10. Create an assault plan. Write down the key terms or formulas you need before you continue. Think how you are going to use the allotted time.

11. If you have time at the end of the exam, go back and reread your work and look again at multiple-choice questions. Check to see that you answered every question before you take the exam. But remember, your first answer is usually the best one. Be extremely careful about changing the answers later on.

12. Do not do lots of different things while studying. Set time to study beforehand and follow through. This means leaving your room for most people and turning off visual/auditory

distractions, including iPods, Facebook, and lyric music.

13. Reward yourself, please. If you've been studying conscientiously for a week or more, you should take a little time to relax before you start your studies again.

14. Carefully read out the directions.

15. Write a brief plan for the essay questions before beginning.

16. Leave to the end the most time-consuming problems, especially the ones with low point values.

17. Concentrate on the matter at hand. If you do the test one step at a time, you will find it far less likely to be overwhelming.

18. If you're stuck on a question, bypass that question. Mark the question off so at the end of the exam you can get back to it.

19. Take a moment to review your test preparation strategy. Take into account what has worked and what needs to be improved. In particular, take a moment to see if your study group was helpful.

20. Complete a mock test. Regularly answer questions on a paper without using your notes? If you complete a mock test 3-4 days weeks before an exam, you'll then know where to focus your studying. Then do the same every week. You may also combat pre-test jitters by demonstrating to yourself what you know. A simple way to conduct a mock test is to ask a friend or classmate to give you an oral quiz based on concepts in the textbook or in either of your notes.

About the SAT

The SAT is a nationally-recognized college entrance examination available to students as part of the college application process. The exam has four sections: English, Mathematics with a calculator, Mathematics without a calculator and Reading. The SAT can have the option of a writing exam, which some colleges require for admission. Not all colleges will require the writing section, but some do, so make sure that you check with your intended institution. The exam typically takes 3 hours and 50 minutes to complete with breaks (or just over 4 hours with the optional writing test). It is offered nationally in October, November, December, March, May and June.

The test is a must for college applications, everybody knows that colleges require you to submit your SAT or SAT score (or both if you choose to). Institutions receive thousands of applications every year the scores on the SAT allow them to narrow the field and make decisions on who they will accept. This also makes your score crucial. The schools that are receiving 75,000 applications don't have time to read every document, transcript, or essay. A low score may automatically count against you, and a high one will work in your favor.

In addition to your college applications, your score can also gain you access to scholarships. These are sometimes merit based scholarships, granted directly from your choice of college during the application process. Others may be from local, state, or regional programs where your grades, academic achievements, and score affect your eligibility.

Your SAT score offers you another opportunity to show the college or university how far you've come academically, even if your GPA is a little lower than expect or want. It's your opportunity to show you can work under pressure, study hard, and perform well. This is a major reason why you should study and be prepared on test day.

Studying and taking the SAT exam can be an extremely daunting task, but, they are extremely important to your future. Your colleges will use them during the early application process to see if you're a strong fit at their school. If you feel you could improve upon the score after your first attempt, try to retake the exam after more practice. A high SAT score will be worth it!

Structure and format

Although it may seem as though it is, sometimes; the SAT is not written by people who want to make you suffer! Instead, the writers each come from different areas, each bringing different skills to the table to help create a test that is a fair but holistic representation of students. The SAT hires high school teachers and college professors for insight into what skills are common in the best students, and how to make questions that can help select these very students. SAT test makers also hire psychologists who have a deep understanding not only of how the brain functions, but specifically how it works under pressure. This is very important so that they can make questions that are both fair and challenging under a time constraint.

The people who write test questions are not out there to get you- instead, they're using their expertise in various fields to create questions that will challenge you to think critically under a time crunch, which is a skill you'll draw on time and time again in college. While the SAT is definitely a necessary evil, understand that there's a lot of time and effort that goes into the questions to make sure the exam is accurate, challenging, and fair.

How to register

You can register for the SAT online or by mail. The SAT recommends registering online because it is faster, you can immediately see if your preferred test center has space available, and you can print your admission ticket immediately after submitting payment.

Registering Online

To register online, you need to create an SAT Web Account, which you can do on the SAT website. Both U.S. and international students can register online.

Once you have created an account, you will be able to register for the SAT. During the registration process, you will be asked questions about your high school, classes, your background, your family and your interests. In addition, you will also need to fill in information such as your name, address, phone number, email, and social security number. Once this is all done, you can proceed to register for the SAT itself.

The registration process will ask you to select your preferred test date, select whether you will take the SAT (No Writing) or the SAT Plus Writing, and it will let you know the price. During the registration process, you will also be able to choose which schools you would like to receive your SAT test scores (although you do not have to select any schools if you prefer not to). You will choose where you'd like to take the SAT, it's important here to sign up early, since testing centers can fill up fast! Finally, you will be asked to confirm all the everything you have written, thus far and then provide a method of payment (credit cards are the only payment method accepted when registering online).

If you register online you will have the ability to print out your SAT score report from your SAT Web Account as soon as scores are available and the report is ready. If you are unable to test on Saturdays (the usual day the SAT is administered) due to religious beliefs, if you are homebound or confined, or if you need to receive testing accommodations due to a disability, you will have to complete additional documentation outside of your SAT Web Account in order to have the test administered to you.

Registering by Mail

Although mail registration is available for everyone, the SAT requires you to register by mail if you are under the age of 13, or if you cannot pay for your registration via credit card.

In order to register by mail, you need to request a registration pack from the SAT. A registration pack will then be mailed to you, and you will have to fill it all in and mail it back. Students requesting non-Saturday testing, accommodated testing, or who are homebound or confined will need to submit additional information.

Why do the SAT

A standardized test can be terrifying, so why would anybody want to do it?

1. Many colleges will need to see your scores. There are, however, some colleges that do not need scores. Most colleges need to see how you did on the ACT or SAT. Colleges will consider only one so you don't have to apply both unless you want to, and no college will decide which one you should send.

2. There are score-based Scholarships. Most colleges award students with a lot of scholarship money, provided they can produce the correct test scores. Taking the SAT (and performing

well on it) could potentially lead to a full ride in some schools and a generous scholarship in many others.

3. Some employers need to see your scores. This may seem strange, and this is definitely a newer phenomenon. Also, some prospective employers want to see data from your SAT before they recruit you. It doesn't only apply to career training, either; it also extends to consultancy and financial sector work. It's becoming more popular, according to the Wall Street Journal.

4. The SAT Essay does not want you to express your opinion, instead it asks you to review and analyze the information you are given.

5. Many states require the SAT: Every high school student attending school in some states must take the form of the SAT, whether or not written. If you live in one of the states in question, there is little choice to make.

Testing Irregularities

A "testing irregularity" is essentially an accusation of cheating. You can and should avoid this wherever possible. To do so: follow all instructions and only work on the section on which you are supposed to be working. This includes marking the answer sheets. Don't go back to a previous section or forward to a later section, however tempting this may be; either in the test book or on the answer sheet. Do write in the test booklet. Sometimes showing your working out can save you from a testing irregularity, and therefore the time and worry that comes with it.

If you are accused of a testing irregularity, don't panic. You have certain rights and you may be able to prove your innocence. Discuss the matter with your parents and perhaps an attorney as soon as possible so that you can respond accordingly.

SAT and ACT Differences and Similarities

At a glance, the two tests aren't that different. Both the ACT and SAT are nationally recognized standardized tests and common admission requirements for US schools. Mainly taken by high school juniors and seniors, each test measures students' ability in lots of critical skill areas—

such as problem solving and reading comprehension. These are skill areas which are required for college success.

The content of the ACT and SAT are more similar now, than before as a since the SAT's massive redesign in 2016. Now, both exams have the following features:

Contain the same sections like Reading, Math, etc. in a predetermined order, with each section appearing just once

Offer an optional essay section whereby the score does not count toward your total.

Use correct answer only scoring, meaning you do not lose marks if you get a question wrong.

Contain passage-based Reading and English/Writing questions (called English on the SAT).

Despite all of this the ACT and SAT have their differences. For one, the ACT takes a little longer than the SAT. On top of this, the number of questions and time limits are different for corresponding sections.

Below is a look at the basic format for both the ACT and SAT:

	ACT	SAT
Time	2 hrs. 55 mins without Writing 3 hrs. 35 mins with Writing	3 hrs. without Essay 3 hrs. 50 mins with Essay
Order	1. English 2. Math 3. Reading 4. Science 5. Writing (optional)	1. Reading 2. Writing and Language 3. Math No Calculator 4. Math Calculator 5. Essay (optional)
Time Per Section	English: 45 mins Math: 60 mins Reading: 35 mins Science: 35 mins Writing (optional): 40 mins	Reading: 65 mins Writing and Language: 35 mins Math No Calculator: 25 mins Math Calculator: 55 mins Essay (optional): 50 mins

Number of Questions	English: 75 questions Math: 60 questions Reading: 40 questions Science: 40 questions Writing (optional): 1 essay	Reading: 52 questions Writing and Language: 44 questions Math No Calculator: 20 questions Math Calculator: 38 questions Essay (optional): 1 essay
Scoring	Total score range: 1-36 Each section uses a scale of 1-36. Your total score is the average of your four section scores. The optional Writing section uses a scale of 2-12 and does not count toward your final score.	Total score range: 400-1600 The Evidence-Based Reading and Writing (EBRW) and Math sections each use a scale of 200-800 and are combined for a total score. The optional Essay uses three separate scales of 1-8 and does not count toward your final score.
Cost	$50.50 without Writing $67.00 with Writing	$47.50 without Essay $64.50 with Essay
Who Accepts Scores?	Accepted by all colleges and universities in the US	Accepted by all colleges and universities in the US

Below you can see the time per question assuming that you spend the same amount of time on each question.

	ACT	SAT
Reading	53 sec/question	75 sec/question
SAT English Writing and Language/SAT Writing	36 sec/question	48 sec/question

Math	60 sec/question	No Calculador: 75 sec/question
		Calculator: 87 sec/question
Science	53 sec/question	N/A
Reading	53 sec/question	75 sec/question

Unlike the ACT, the SAT does give you some formulas on test day, meaning you don't need to memorize all potential formulas before taking the test.

Another difference between the two tests deals with essay content. On both the SAT and ACT, the essay component is optional; however, what you must write about differs depending on whether you're taking the SAT or ACT.

On the SAT, you'll be given a passage, which you must read and then analyze. Your essay will dissect the author's argument using evidence and reasoning. In other words, you will *not* be giving your own opinion.

Here's an example of an SAT Essay prompt:

As you read the passage below, consider how "The Author" uses evidence, such as facts or examples, to support claims. Reasoning to develop ideas and to connect claims and evidence.

Stylistic or persuasive elements, such as word choice or appeals to emotion, to add power to the ideas expressed.

Which essay type is easier for you depends on what you're better at and more comfortable with writing. With the SAT, you'll need to have good reading comprehension skills in order to fully realize the strengths and weaknesses of the author's argument.

SAT vs ACT: Which Test Is Right for You?

If you're not sure which of the SAT or ACT tests you want to take, here are 3 methods you could use to help you decide.

Method 1: Take Official Practice Tests

The best way to decide between the ACT and SAT is to actually take each test and then compare your scores. To do this, you'll need to find practice tests for both the ACT and SAT. Choose one official practice test for each exam and then decide when you're going to take them. They both take about four hours, so make sure you set aside enough time to complete each test without interruption. Do not take the tests on the same day or even two days in a row. In addition, make sure that you're taking the tests in a quiet place and are timing yourself correctly.

Do both practice tests, then calculate your SAT and ACT scores using your practice tests' respective scoring guides and then compare your scores.

If your SAT and ACT scores are nearly or exactly the same, you'll probably perform equally well on either test. So, it's up to you, then, to decide whether you'd like to try taking both tests, or whether you'd rather just take one.

Method 2: Take an SAT vs ACT Quiz

Another option which is significantly quicker would be to take the quiz below:

Statement	Agree	Disagree
I find geometry and trigonometry hard.		
Math problems in my head without a calculator are easy.		
I do not do well on Science questions.		
I am better at analysis and evaluation than giving my own thoughts.		
I score highly on math tests.		
I don't like learning formulas by rote.		

I like writing my own answers for math questions rather than multi choice answers.		
I get stressed when the pressure is on due to the clock		
I can normally justify my thoughts with evidence.		
I prefer chronological questions		

Now, count up your check marks in each column to find out what your score means.

A. Mostly Agrees — The SAT

If you agreed with most or all of the above points, then the SAT is the exam you should do.

B. Mostly Disagrees — The ACT

If you disagreed with most or all of the above, you'll most likely choose to do the ACT rather than the SAT. On the SAT, you won't need to think of your own answers to math problems, and you get to state your opinion when you're writing.

C. Equal - Either test will work!

If you're equal in your scores then both the SAT and ACT will suit you. In this case you should rely on method 1 or method 3 to make your decision.

Method 3: Consider Your State's Testing Requirements

Finally, it's important to check if your state has any specific testing requirements. Some states require all students to take the SAT or ACT. In these cases, it's usually best to stick with whatever test is required for your state so that you don't need to study for the other test, too.

There are 11 states that require the ACT:

- Alabama

- Hawaii

- Kentucky
- Mississippi
- Montana
- Nebraska
- Nevada
- North Carolina
- Utah
- Wisconsin
- Wyoming

And there are 10 states/regions that require the SAT:

- Colorado
- Connecticut
- Delaware
- District of Columbia
- Illinois
- Maine
- Michigan
- New Hampshire
- Rhode Island
- West Virginia

Strategies

I will go through each subsection independently but there are some general strategies you should apply throughout preparation for your SAT.

General SAT Testing Strategies

The following are the general strategies for making sure that your overall performance on the SAT is good. These tips and strategies can be applied to all sections in the SAT.

Don't cram - The SAT tests you on knowledge you've accumulated over the course of your high school career, so there's no point in cramming. The day before the test, take it easy, watch a movie and then get a good night's sleep. Staying up the night before the test and studying will only stress you out and cause you to be tired the next day hence having a negative impact on performance.

Familiarize yourself with the test - Become familiar with the layout and format of the SAT before the actual day on which you sit it. During your test prep, learn and review the directions for each of the sections on the test. When you arrive, be prepared for what will arise in each section of the SAT. This will save valuable time during the test which can be spent working on questions.

Answer as many easy questions as you can; First - Answer the questions you're sure you know the correct answer to first. Go through the exam book, put a mark next to each question you skip so you can quickly find them later. After you've done the easy ones, go back and take on the more difficult questions.

Write in your test booklet; The SAT test booklet is yours. After the test it will be thrown in the trash. This means you should not worry about making sure it remains in mint condition. Use it. Write in it, cross out wrong answers and use it to do scratch work. Work out issues and jot down key information you'll need to answer certain questions, this is really useful for when you're struggling.

Don't, however, write on your answer sheet - your SAT answer sheet is scored by a computer. This computer is not able to tell the difference between a correct answer, a stray mark, or a sketch in the margin. Make sure that your answer sheet is marked correctly, neatly and free of any stray marks. Follow the directions given carefully as you mark correct answers on your answer sheet.

There is only one correct answer. On the SAT, there is only one correct answer to each question. Even if it appears as if there are two correct answers, you can only choose one answer – so select the best answer to each question. With this in mind, be wary of red herrings, sent to catch you out.

Guess. If you're faced with a hard question and you don't know the correct answer, just make an educated guess. Try to delete as many answer choices as you can, particularly if they're obviously incorrect and then select the answer that makes the most sense. There are no marks lost for wrong answers therefore it is always worth putting an answer down.

Be careful with your time. You must make sure that you do not spend lots of time on any one question. There is a time limit for completing the test, and it is easy to get held up in one question and therefore not even be able to access some easy questions. It is best to limit yourself to a set amount of time per question, with a small addition for harder questions, and a subtractionfor easier ones. If you run out of this time on the question, skip it. There are easy marks on the paper and you don't want to miss them through being stuck in one question. The SAT consists of 4-5 small mini-tests that are timed. Pay close attention to how much time remains in each section, so you will not have to rush at the last minute to complete each test. Bring a watch or stopwatch that you can use for this on the test day, and use the same device when practicing.

Read each question very carefully. Until you have read a question in its entirety do not assume you know what it is asking. Sometimes students will give an answer they recall from a similar question from a practice test. Read the words to each question carefully.

Don't change your answers unless you're sure you made an error. Most of the time you would be better off sticking with your first choice.

Finally, do lots of practice. With any exam; practice is key!

English Writing and Language Section Strategies

The English section of the SAT consists of 44-questions, and is a 35-minute test. not a lot of time per question, so you'll need to work fast in order to complete this section.

The English section has passages, which are followed by a selection of multiple-choice questions. These questions are designed to test your reading comprehension and may ask about specific content (sentences, phrases, concepts, etc.) covered in each passage. Several questions will test Usage and Mechanics (including grammar, sentence structure, punctuation and usage). Other questions will test Rhetorical Skills (organization, strategy, and style). You'll receive a score for your performance in each of these two categories.

Punctuation questions will test your understanding of internal and end-of sentence grammatical conventions. Grammar and Usage questions test your understanding of basic grammar rules. Sentence Structure questions test your understanding of the relationship between clauses in order to link clauses and form sentences. The Strategy questions are designed to test your ability to choose correct words and phrases within the context of an essay or passage. Organization questions test your ability to organize ideas and choose correct sentence structures within the context of a passage or essay. Style questions will test your ability to select the most appropriate words and sentence structures to maintain or support the style and tone of an essay.

On Punctuation questions you should read, review and consider the entire sentence, even if the question is asking you to focus on just a subset of the sentence. When answering SAT English Writing and Language questions, never focus on just part of the sentence. You must make sure your answer makes sense within the context of the entire sentence and passage.

When answering Grammar questions, read each question, and read it very carefully to be sure that you don't make mistakes. It's easy to select the wrong answer, even when you understand the concept, if you don't read the question carefully and understand what is being requested.

For Organization questions, find the choice that makes the most sense when put in front the first sentence of the passage.

For Strategy questions think about the whole thing and decide whether a suggested change makes it clearer or not.

When answering Sentence Structure questions, look at the sentence as a complete sentence and then decide if an answer choice offers the most natural and clear relationship.

To answer Style questions correctly you need to understand the meaning and tone.

Pay attention to the style of the writing. The correct answer will suit the individual author's style than other choices.

Carefully examine each answer option to see how they differ from one another.

If "No change" is a possible answer, only choose it if other options are wrong. This can be a dangerous choice if you aren't familiar with obscure grammar rules. Double check all other answers before selecting "no change". (Note: The "no change" answer is the correct answer about 25-30% of the time so please don't ignore it, it is a genuine choice that should be taken into account).

When given a selection of answers to choose from, try and insert each of the options into the sentence to see which one fits the best.

In questions with underlined text, check all the sentences around it to figure out how these sentences relate to the underlined section. Then, compare the answer you've selected with the underlined text.

Reading Section Strategies

The Reading section of the SAT is a 52-question, 65-minute test that covers passages of text followed by answer choices. The passages can include Prose Fiction/Literary Narrative, Social Science, Humanities, and Natural Science.

Prose Fiction and Literary Narrative passages contain excerpts from literary and fiction texts. This section will ask you questions about the main theme of the passage, the narrator's tone and intent, the message of the passage, and which questions are or are not answered in the passage.

Social Science passages typically offer a straightforward discussion of social science topics, including sociology, education, and psychology, among others. You'll get questions about the main point of the passage, the author's view, and how information presented supports the subject of the passage.

Humanities passages often come from personal essays and memoirs, and address subjects such as literature, art, philosophy, or media. You'll likely be asked questions about the tone of the passage and point of view of the narrator.

Natural Science passages are nonfiction passages about science. They will cover all sorts of subjects, including biology, chemistry, technology, physics, or medicine. Questions often focus on specifics which must be supported by the text. This seems like a lot of content and enough to strike fear into students, but worry not; with the correct strategies you will be fine.

You need to focus on crucial information to answer each question as you read the passage. To do so: read the question first! - before you read the text.

Be very careful when you read the text. focus on the main points of the passage and try not to get distracted by the details - as you may not need the detail that distracts you, when you come to the final answer.

Eliminate incorrect answer choices. All incorrect answers have incorrect options that you could choose. If you can pick out and remove all of the incorrect options, you will be left with the correct option. Which sounds simple!

Start with your strongest passage topic. If you're competent in Science then start with the Natural Science passage.

Employ a 3-stage method (previewing, reading and reviewing) to improve your comprehension and understanding of each passage. As you read each passage, focus on the big ideas.

Take short notes as you read each paragraph focusing on the purpose of the passage. Keep track of the various people and opinions within the text, and refer to your notes when answering.

Frequently check back with the passage when determining correct answers. Make sure your answer is supported by the text.

Mathematics Sections Strategies

The mathematics section is broken up into two papers, calculator and none calculator. The no calculator section is 25 minutes long and 20 questions long. The calculator section is 38 questions and 55 minutes long. Both tests are designed to test the math skills and knowledge you've acquired over your time in high school. The content covered in the SAT mathematics test includes: Number & Quantity, Algebra, Functions, Geometry, Statistics & Probability, Integrating Essential Skills and Modeling.

It is advisable in this section to work out the answer before looking at the answers available to you. If none of the answer options match yours, redo the problem.

Calculators are usually only useful to compute figures. Do not rely too heavily on a calculator during the calculator section since you will have to work problems out to effectively solve them. If you don't understand how to approach a problem or use formulas a calculator won't be much help.

When possible, make a prediction as to what you believe the answer will be. If the final answer is completely different from your prediction, redo the problem, you may have made an error.

Once you have gotten to the answer, move on to the next problem. You have less than 60 seconds to answer each question. Always double check your calculations. When you rush it is easy to make mistakes.

The general instructions on the math portion of the SAT are fairly long. Read these instructions and become familiar with them the day before the test. Don't waste time reading these instructions on the day of the test.

Use the same method to approach every SAT math question. (1) Read the question. (2) Review the information provided in the question and the answer options. (3) Solve the question by back solving, picking numbers, using traditional math, or strategically guessing. (4) Make sure you answered the specific question being asked. To save time, back solve when you can. Back solving problems works when you see integers in the answer choices.

As you reach each question, translate the words into math and make notes as you go. It is much easier to see it written in math than in lots of wordy problems. This way you can more easily identify and solve the problem. Don't forget that "of" indicates multiplication is required.

Go back through your high school math and study number properties (odd, even, prime, and order of operation), triangles (30-60-90 and 45-45-90 rules, pythagorean triplets 3:4:5, 5:12:13 and their multiples), common shapes and math relationships (values, ratios, and percents).

Watch out for "trap" answers. These include answers that are way off the mark, and clearly incorrect. Identifying trap answers will help you narrow your selection of answer options, if you can remove a few from a question your chances of getting it correct have vastly improved.

Essay Prompt Strategies

The SAT writing Section is a 50-minute essay test. This test is designed to measure your ability to write at a high school and pre-college level.

My advice is to use the 5-paragraph essay format (introduction, thesis statement, supporting paragraphs, and conclusion), in the writing section.

Make a plan of your route before each writing task.

Make the main points of your essay and don't digress into other points. Stick to your point.

To support your comments, use details and examples, make them as clear as possible.

Your handwriting must be neat and readable. Make sure that it is easy to understand and that whilst your language and vocab is professional, it should be easy to understand.

Make it abundantly clear what your opinion is and how it relates to the three perspectives provided.

Explain every point you make, completely. Use examples to make your point clearer.

Make sure your response is organized in a logical way. Give each point you make 1-2 paragraphs.

Make sure your word choice is skillful, precise and your sentences are clear. This does not mean you have to use fancy vocabulary or words rather that every sentence you should not add confusion but should make it easier to understand the point which you are making.

Remember that how you score will depend on your writing style and skill not on your knowledge. If you can write well, you will score well

Your essay should be at least one page in length. A page and half is a good target length of your essay however, make sure not to repeat yourself.

At the end your essays for spelling, grammar, errors if you can.

Psychology in examinations

This section will help you prepare for all exams, how to manage stress levels and not freak out in the exam hall.

If you're one of the many people who gets stressed out when it comes to taking exams then I have a few tips for you that will help you to overcome this and really concentrate on achieving good grades.

Stress Management

Firstly, look after your health. It's too easy to cram so much information into your brain and also try to get on with the rest of your life. You'll end up burning the candle at both ends, so to speak, and this can seriously damage your health.

Looking after your health means that you should be getting adequate rest. Eat and drink sensibly and in moderation, exercise your body and spend quality time on yourself.

Studying at every available opportunity can lead to information overload. Make yourself a program and stick to it as much as possible. Studying for 20 minutes at a time, followed by a 'reflection period' on what you have learned and then a 10 minute break - is ideal for optimum learning. We all have a shorter attention span than we think, so use this logic to maximize the attention that you have.

Make your learning fun. If you have someone to study with then use the opportunity to test each other on what you've learned so far, when you're away from your books. Forming a study group can really help with this.

If you find your mind begins to wander during your work then there's no point in continuing at this time with your learning because your brain won't absorb the information as easily as it would if you were at your peak. Take a break, then return.

Practice relaxation exercises. Meditation is an excellent way to control your mindset in an exam. There are lots of free apps that can help you with some basic relaxation techniques if you find that you get stressed.

Do one thing at a time. Decide which Topic you're going to study and don't change it. If you get interrupted, put the interruption to one side until you're ready to deal with it.

Day of the exam

It's always useful to have a routine and fall backs for the day of the exam, if you're well prepared and feeling comfortable then you are in the right place to do well!

Physical Strategies

Sleep: Get enough sleep the night before the exam. If you're foggy because of a lack of sleep, you will not be able to perform at your best. Sleep a few extra hours instead of studying a few extra hours.

Food: Eat moderately before your exams; avoid a heavy meal. If you eat too much, your brain will spend energy on the digestion of the food. On the other hand, if you skip a meal altogether, your brain will have inadequate fuel to function well. Aim for nutritional balance and moderation, if you practicethis in advance, for practicetests and the like, then you will be prepared.

Alcohol: Any easy mistake to make, but obvious, don't drink the night before your exam. Alcohol upsets the chemical balance in your body and affects the way your brain functions. It could also give you a hangover, which would be a real nuisance on exam day!

Drinks: With this in mind also avoid drinking diuretics that contain caffeine such as coffee, tea or cola, which could make you need to use the washroom more often, you want to make the most of all the time you have.

Water: Your body and your brain need water. Research has proven that your brain performs more efficiently when well-hydrated. Drink enough water, but not so much that you need to use the bathroom.

Temperature: The aim is to be as comfortable as possible during your exam so that you are not distracted. Take a sweater or jacket along in case of excessive air-conditioning or lack of sufficient heating. Choose a seat near a window for fresh air, if possible, but also avoid the window if there is a lot of noise outside. Arriving early may allow you to select the seat you feel most comfortable in.

Breathing: Deep breathing involves breathing slowly and deeply. Start by inhaling through your nose. You will find this to be relaxing. Try to make sure your chest isn't rising and falling, rather; expand your belly with each breath, while your chest remains still. Try to reach a count of 6 on each in breath, and 6 on each out breath. When you have mastered this process, you can add a pause of 6 seconds between the inhaling and exhaling breath.

Brain Gym techniques are worth looking at: This program of simple exercises can enhance learning and performance by improving the brain's neural pathways. Students of all ages have achieved higher test scores after engaging in a short brain gym session. Learn more about these simple techniques and give yourself an edge.

Psychological Techniques

Positive Visualization: This is a powerful psychological technique that can be used to enhance your positive feelings and diminish the negative ones. It is based on the fact that the mind and body are powerfully interconnected. You can create changes in your heart rate, skin temperature, and brainwave patterns by the thoughts you have. You can use this information to your advantage before and during your SAT. Imagine yourself doing really well; see yourself getting the score you need for your college, recalling the information easily and remaining calm and in control.

Handling Anxiety: Practice deep breathing techniques if you find yourself becoming nervous or overwhelmed. By breathing correctly, you can give your brain fuel to help it perform better. Arrive early: This will help you avoid unnecessary stress in the immediate period before your exam. Allow for traffic, check the weather reports for exam day, or even travel to an external exam location in advance to get an idea of how long it will take you to travel there on the day of the exam.

Avoid other nervous test takers: While waiting for the exam to begin, avoid speaking to any nervous students and taking on their negative energy. If you can: remain confident and focused on doing well on the exam.

Bring necessary materials: Keep extra materials such as pens, pencils, calculators, rulers, or compasses packed and ready the night before the exam so you have time to locate or even purchase any misplaced or lost items. Knowing you have everything you need will make you feel calmer and well-prepared.

Mental Strategies for the day of the exam

Review output: If you have some time before the exam, use it to review material and practiceyour output. Don't try to learn new material at this stage.

Stay for the entire exam: Stay for the full length of the exam. Even if you feel you cannot recall any more, by relaxing or waiting in the exam hall, information and details might come to mind and enable you to score additional points. On exams, every point counts.

Make sure you focus on reading the Instructions really carefully, preferably in advance. This is the most common avoidable mistake made by students. Don't let it happen to you. It's also worth knowing what the instructions for each section will be, in advance, that way you don't need to read them in detail and waste time on the exam day.

Read each question: Really read what you are being asked to do on each question. Don't presume it's the angle you're familiar with. Go back through it to see what you're Actuallybeing asked and remember that exams change all the time, so questions that appeared in the past may differ from those given in the present.

Focus on you: Don't look around at how other students are doing. For one thing it may appear that you're trying to cheat. If nothing else it will distract you from your main task which is to do as well as possible on your exams.

Budget your time: Check how much each question counts towards your final mark and spend time on each answer accordingly. If you have a choice to write your answers in any order, do the easy ones first to build up your confidence.

How to take the SAT

The following section is a summary of how to perform at your very best on the at of the SAT. Much like any sporting event, an exam is a single day's performance that can vary, depending on a multitude of factors. As such the following will help you maximize your performance on the day.

Your SAT test day should be viewed in four sections

- Before you leave your house
- At the test center
- During the test
- After the test

Before you leave your house on SAT test day

1. First of all, be sure to finish your studying for the test the night before you take it.

    When you wake up in the morning, you don't want to have to worry about something you don't understand. Get all of your studying done in plenty of time, if you aren't sure about something on the day, leave it. The stress of panicking to study last minute will outweigh the gain. If there are any formulas or last minute tips that you want to be sure you're able to remember, write these down on a piece of paper that you can bring with you and look at on your way to the testing center—but remember, you cannot use this piece of paper during the exam.

2. Be sure to get plenty of sleep the night before you take the SAT.

Try to get at least eight hours of sleep, and be sure to factor in the time that it might take you to fall asleep and the time you might lose as a result of nervousness over the exam. Nobody performs at their best when they are exhausted, so do what you can to avoid being in that exact situation.

3. If you're particularly worried about being well-rested enough for the exam, it can help to plan out how early you will need to wake up and then count your sleep-cycles backwards so that you will wake up feeling refreshed. There are plenty of apps that will help you with this if you want to. Google is your friend here. Make sure, if you do decide to plot your sleep schedule: that you get started with it weeks if not months before the SAT so you are familiar with the app, and with the whole process.

4. Plan out your clothes the night before the exam.

    It should be something comfortable. It should also be something professional. Showing up in a professional outfit or an outfit will make you feel more prepared to take the test. Get it ready the night before the exam so that you can just wake up and get dressed first thing in the morning. Take a shower if you usually do or if it helps you get started with your day. Also be sure to pack a bag filled with everything that you need. This way in the morning, you have much less distractions.

5. With this in mind: Make sure that you stick to your morning routine the morning of the test so that your brain isn't busy making decisions. You should be walking into the testing center with a fresh mind. It also might be helpful to read something light and easy beforehand to get your brain warmed up a little bit. It is important to stress the light and easy bit. You wouldn't sprint 100 yards before running a marathon race, but you may go for a short jog to get the blood flowing - it's the same logic here.

6. For some students, it is helpful to have a ritual.

    Before a big test, you might want to think of something specific that you could do for good luck, such as wearing a favorite pair of socks to the testing center, listening to your favorite song, or saying a special mantra before taking the exam. While this "good luck charm" doesn't have anything to do with the actual test, it can be nice to do something special that will make you feel comfortable and boost your confidence. Many athletes and successful business people follow this exactroutine, so why not you!

At the testing center

7. Arrive at the testing center early and go to the bathroom, even if you don't think you need to!

    You don't want to have to rush to the testing center in case there is traffic, and you also don't want to be distracted while taking the exam because you need to use the bathroom. It will be helpful to use the bathroom before the exam, so if you do need to go during a break, you will know where it is and the fastest way to get to it.

8. If you have last-minute questions, consult your sheet on which you wrote down last minute tips.

    Don't strain yourself too much trying to memorize, you already know your stuff, and if you don't, now is not the time, all you will achieve is getting more stressed. Rather than scrambling to take in information at the last minute, it is more important that you get in the right mindset to take the test and remain calm and composed. This will be far more beneficial than the alternative.

During the test

9. Stay Calm. Practice the breathing techniques discussed earlier.

10. Bring a cold bottle of water with you—while you can't actually eat or drink anything while you're taking the exam, you can drink and snack during breaks.

    Staying hydrated will avoid tiredness which is often a result of dehydration. Don't drink too much water, though, because you don't want to have to use the bathroom in the middle of the exam!

11. Utilize your breaks during the exam efficiently.

    Move around so that your body and mind can sustain themselves for the next section of the exam, stretch, go to the bathroom, look out the window, or eat a snack!

After the test

12. When you are done taking the SAT, write down any areas of difficulty that you encountered.

    Even though you will get a detailed score report that will tell you the areas on which you did well on and which ones you might need to improve, it's also useful to go through a stage of reflection. You can later compare this to your actual scores. This will also be helpful in case you want to study for the test again before you even get your score report back.

13. Once you finish the exam, go outside and do something fun.

    Relax and forget about the test. Take the rest of the day off. Do something that you enjoy doing. You'll certainly have time to think more about it later (especially when you receive your score report). For now, it is most important that you have fun, remain balanced, and congratulate yourself on getting through a long, hard testing day.

Guessing/Process of elimination

Although content mastery is the best way to get a great SAT score, there are key testing strategies that perfect-scorers use to tilt the odds in their favor. Some of these strategies are secret, and others are well-known. But, one of the oldest and most dependable testing strategies of all time, is the process of elimination.

The process of elimination is a classic strategy that should and will be used on standardized tests and multiple-choice quizzes for the rest of time.

On the SAT, proper use of the process of elimination starts before you start crossing answers off.

By which, I mean that you should answer the question before you begin using elimination, for maximum effectiveness. Otherwise you'll just be eliminating answer choices based on your "feelings." Experience proves that this is risky, and will cost you points on the SAT.

So, before you attempt to eliminate, start by answering the question don't forget to write it down, too.

Now, as you move onto the Elimination phase, it's important to ignore your gut instinct. What you should do is to find the errors that mean that you can eliminate an answer choice.

If you just eliminate an answer choice because you "don't feel like it's this one," then you might as well be guessing. The process of elimination is not guesswork, it is removal of known incorrect answers.

Remember that any error, no matter how minor, makes the whole answer choice wrong! As you develop your skills of Elimination on the SAT, you will learn to notice the errors hidden in each answer choice. Once you start noticing these, you really won't be able stop noticing them!

It takes practice and time to reach this point where you can spot the errors easily. The key is in being accurate but still finishing on time.

Note: As a strategy, the process of elimination is less effective on Math questions. Although there is a use for elimination on Math, it's better to just do the question. Techniques you learn from your math teacher or tutor would be the most effective, and the fastest.

So, instead of trying to forcibly eliminate your way to correct Math answers, study your SAT Math skills. Save the heavy-duty usage of the process of elimination for the other sections.

The process of elimination works well on the SAT because they are designed to trick you. This is most true in the verbal sections, particularly the Reading sections of the SAT.

In the Verbal sections, the SAT deliberately uses words to trick and deceive you. Fake answer choices are carefully crafted with deceptive keywords. Many times, the wrong answer is actually true - it's just irrelevant.

As I said in the beginning of this book, the SAT is different to most other tests you take in high school. Most of your teachers in high school classes don't want to trick you, they just want to test you. But, the SAT does want to do exactly this!

Mistakes that you can make with the process of elimination:

- Trying to eliminate before you Pre-Answer.

- Not writing down your final answer.

- Finding that your final answer seems flawed but sticking with it regardless.

- Not eliminating all choices going with a gut instinct before the process of elimination is completely finished.

- Spending unnecessary time using Elimination due to lack of practice.

- Using the process of elimination too much in math sections - it's much better to just know how the math problem is supposed to work.

- Elimination is a fantastic strategy for higher SAT scores, but it has downsides as well. You must understand the strengths and weaknesses of the Elimination strategy through hours of practice.

- Every powerful technique has corresponding limitations. The only way to confidently work past those barriers is to gain experience through mindful practice. Understand this as you practice Elimination on the SAT tests.

Summary

Of course, the above strategies really help you in the SAT. They will improve the score that you will get. However, it is also incredibly important that you prepare for each section of the SAT properly as well. The above strategies will only support a detailed study program, not replace it.

SAT English Writing and Language

The SAT English Writing and Language test consists of 44 questions that must be answered within the 35-minute time limit. Below you can find more detailed information about the content and skills these questions test, as well as sample SAT English Writing and Language questions and answer explanations.

SAT English Writing and Language Test Question Types

Questions	
Skills/Content Tested	**Examples**
Punctuation	commas, apostrophes, colons, semicolons, dashes, periods, question marks, and exclamation points
Grammar & Usage	subject-verb agreement, pronoun agreement, pronoun forms and cases, adjectives, adverbs, verb forms, comparative and superlative modifiers, and idioms
Sentence Structure	subordinate or dependent clauses, run-on or fused sentences, comma splices, sentence fragments, misplaced modifiers, shifts in verb tense or voice, and shifts in pronoun person or number
Strategy	adding, revising, or deleting sentences; how a sentence fits with the purpose, audience, and focus of a paragraph or the essay as a whole
Organization	opening, transitional, and closing phrases or statements; order and focus of sentences or paragraphs
Style	writing style, tone, clarity, and effectiveness; eliminating ambiguity, wordiness, and redundant material; clarifying vague or awkward material

The SAT English Writing and Language tests a variety of writing skills from fundamental grammar to effective written communication. This test section involves five passages which will all contain some mistakes. The SAT English Writing and Language test asks the person taking the test to edit the documents, as appropriate.

The SAT English Writing and Language test covers the full range of editorial skills in a multiple-choice format, but does not require students to know technical grammatical terms, instead SAT uses Reporting Categories to provide a more granular analysis of performance. SAT English Writing and Language Reporting Categories detail what students are tested on in this section:

Conventions of Standard English questions measure understanding of the conventions of Standard English grammar, usage, and mechanics. This reporting category focuses on Usage, Punctuation, and Sentence Structure and Formation.

Production of Writing questions measure understanding of the purpose and focus of a piece of writing. This reporting category focuses on Topic Development and Organization, Unity, and Cohesion.

Knowledge of Language questions focus on the use of word choice to make a passage more precise or concise, or to improve syntax, style, or tone.

Because this section is timed, the SAT English Writing and Language section also tests your ability to read quickly and general test taking skills as mentioned earlier in the book.

Sample SAT English Writing and Language Test Questions

To give you a better feel for the format and content of the SAT English Writing and Language test, below there are some sample test questions that you may face.

Usage/Mechanics Question

Determine which answer choice is the best version of the underlined portion of the sentence. If the original is the best version, select "NO CHANGE."

Fitzgerald attended <u>St. Paul Academy; his first</u> published story ran in his school newspaper.

    A. NO CHANGE

B. St. Paul Academy; his first

C. St. Paul Academy, his first

D. St. Paul Academy, but his first

Answer: This question tests a student's knowledge of run-on sentences and punctuation rules. The original sentence fuses two independent clauses without proper punctuation. Due to the fact that there is an error in the original version of the underlined portion of the sentence, we can eliminate choice A. Choice C creates a new error: a comma splice. Two independent clauses cannot be connected by just a comma. Though choice D corrects the run-on sentence error, the addition of the conjunction "but," which implies a contrast, does not fit within the context of the sentence. Choice B, which connects the two independent clauses with a semicolon, correctly fixes the run-on sentence error without creating new errors. Thus, choice B is the correct answer.

Rhetorical Skills Question

Though many high-ranking government and military officials anticipated the possibility of war with Japan, the attack on Pearl Harbor came as a shock to the general population of Oahu, Hawaii. On the morning of December 7th, two Army operators at a radar station picked up the signal of Japanese fighter planes approaching Pearl Harbor. Finally, a low-ranking officer dismissed their report, assuming that the signal must have come from American planes off the west coast of the United States.

Which of the following, if inserted to replace the underlined portion ("Finally,"), would provide the most effective transition between the previous sentence ("On the morning of...") and this one ("Finally, a low-ranking officer...")?

A. NO CHANGE

B. And,

C. However,

D. But,

Answer: When we consider the possible answer choices and the paragraph as a whole, we see that choices A, B, and D do not create an effective transition between the two sentences. We need a transitional word that shows that though there were warning signs of the Pearl Harbor attack, those warnings were not heeded, which is one of the reasons why the attack was such a shock to the general population. Choice C ("However,") would provide the most effective transition. Therefore, choice C is the correct answer.

General Strategies

The SAT English Writing and Language Section will test grammatical and rhetorical concepts in ways that are designed to trip you up. As you can see above, It's not enough to simply choose the answer that "sounds right." In fact, many of the answers that "sound right" are included in order to trip you (as discussed in the early sections of this book).

1. Punctuation.

Punctuation is by far the most important SAT grammar rule.

- Punctuation (commas, apostrophes, dashes, etc.)
- Subject/Verb agreement and Pronoun/Number agreement
- Idioms
- Wrong words (affect/effect, their/they're, etc.)
- Parallel construction
- Verb tenses and conjugations
- Run-on sentences and sentence fragments
- Misplaced modifiers
- Pronoun choice
- Sentence organization
- Tone/Mood
- Author's intent
- Relevance of sentences
- Word choice

2. Avoid Redundancy and Wordiness.

Redundancy questions are very common on the SAT English Writing and Language test. Redundancy means words or phrases that are unnecessary and can be eliminated without affecting the sentence's meaning. The SAT typically includes two different types that you should be aware of: two synonyms used to describe something and implied phrases that don't add anything to the sentence. The best thing to do in these situations is to remember to keep it short and simple and get rid of words that do not add value.

For example:

"Joanne is an outgoing and sociable person."

This sentence uses "outgoing" and "sociable" to describe Joanne, but these words are synonyms so one of them can be removed to avoid redundancy.

Similarly, another example of redundancy could look like this:

"The campers were terrified to come across a giant bear that towered over them."

Again, avoiding redundancy, we can take out the phrase "towered over them" since it is implied by the adjective "giant":

"The campers were terrified to come across a giant bear."

Just remember: keep sentences short and grammatically correct to avoid redundancy.

3. Don't choose the "NO CHANGE" too easily.

In SAT English Writing and Language, you should choose the "NO CHANGE" answer option if you can't detect anything wrong with the sentence. But this comes with a warning, "NO CHANGE" can be an easy option if you can't see anything immediately wrong with the grammar or syntax. But you need to be more careful than that. Make sure you're evaluating the grammar of the sentence and not just listening to how it sounds in your head. If you really think it's "NO CHANGE," double-check the answer choices to be sure. It can be the correct answer, but only one in four times, on average; don't over use it!

4. **As I said in the earlier sections, practiceis key. Do as much as you can.**

It's not enough to just study grammar rules and read tips and strategies from a review book like this! It's also important to take practice tests:

- Get you used to the format of the test
- Show you the types of questions you can expect to see
- Get you familiar with the instructions

5. **Find Your Weaknesses.**

In order to do really well, you need to find your weakest area, and focus on that. There's no point doing questions that you find the easiest over and over again. You need to improve on the questions you find hard. To do this, keep a note of all the questions that you either guess on, or get wrong. These are the questions on which you are weakest. Then, when you have the list. Use it to study. Go through the questions, search out similar questions, and seek support!

6. **Make Grammar a Part of Your Everyday Life.**

Don't think of grammar as requirement of exams only, think of it as an essential life skill. To do this, you need to make grammar a part of your everyday life.

For example, you can:

- Look out for grammar mistakes in brochures, posters, grocery store signs, etc.
- Proofread your friends' essays and let them know that you're going to be brutal.
- Start posting, tweeting, texting, and messaging with a higher standard of grammar and punctuation.
- Read novels, formal publications, reports, anything of a high standard, so that you are witnessing good grammar, often.
- Look through some of your old essays and improve them.
- Follow grammar-related social media (there are plenty - google it).

7. **Pace Yourself and Leave Extra Time to Check Your Work.**

This is no different to the advice given earlier, but it is equally important here.

If you have time, go back and check on a third time. Ignore the questions you're 100% sure about and focus on the questions you're still struggling with. In the last two minutes before the test is over, quickly go through and make sure you answered every question and filled them out correctly on the bubble sheet.

8. Know the Four Most Common Question Types.

The SAT may be difficult, but it's repeatable. You should know the following common questions:

I. **Using correct punctuation:** Identify which punctuation mark should be used (comma, apostrophe, semicolon, colon, dash, parenthesis, etc.) and where it should go in the sentence.

II. **Choosing the correct form or word:** Identify the best word to use in the sentence. Some questions might ask you to find the right form of the word, such as correct verb tense, singular or plural, correct pronoun, correct preposition, or correct idiom.

III. **Logic questions:** Choose the answer that expresses the correct relationship between two parts of the sentence, paragraph, or passage (conjunction, where a sentence should go, the relevance of a sentence, etc.)

IV. **Finding the main idea and interpreting a passage:** Identify the main purpose or point of the passage, sentence, or paragraph.

Grammar rules

While you read through the essays, you don't need to remember every grammar rule. Instead, think about the common grammar rules that are likely to come up on the exam. By focusing on what you know you'll see, you can increase your score while reducing the amount of time and energy you spend on each question. These are likely to be:

1. Run-Ons & Fragments

A complete sentence contains a subject, a predicate verb, and a complete thought. If any of the three is lacking, the sentence is called a fragment. A run-on contains too much information, usually because two independent clauses (two complete thoughts) are being improperly combined.

2. Verbs: Subject-Verb Agreement & Verb Tenses

The SAT English Writing and Language Section often includes long sentences in which the main subject and the verb are separated by many words or clauses. If you identify the subject of each sentence and make sure the verb matches it, you can ace this grammar rule. In addition, the SAT tests your knowledge of past, present, future, past perfect, present perfect, and future perfect tenses.

3. Punctuation

Commas, apostrophes, colons, semicolons, dashes, periods, question marks, and exclamation points are all tested on the SAT. Know how to tackle them to grab some quick points on this test.

4. Idioms

Idioms are expressions native to the English language. Two-part idioms are commonly tested such as "neither...nor" and "not only...but also" as well as prepositional idioms like "opposed TO" and "participate IN." The SAT will also test verb and preposition idioms. Both of these types can be tricky because there is not a list of rules. Instead of trying to memorize each one, you should practice to get a sense of which idioms come up frequently.

5. Wordiness

As long as there are no new grammar errors introduced, the shortest answer choice is often correct. Redundancy is a type of wordiness where the same thing is said twice such as "happy and joyful." Keep it simple and to the point.

6. Parallel Structure

Parallelism is tested on the SAT English Writing and Language test in the context of phrases or items in a list. In parallel construction, the phrases or items must be in the same form. This can be tested with a number of parts of speech: nouns, verbs, prepositions, etc.

7. Pronouns

The most common error associated with pronouns is pronoun-antecedent agreement. The antecedent is the word the pronoun is replacing. A pronoun *must* have a clear antecedent in the sentence. Sometimes the antecedent is present, but will disagree with the pronoun in number. A less common error is the ambiguous pronoun in which a pronoun could represent more than one noun. For example, "The president and his adviser spoke for hours before he reached a decision." The pronoun 'he' could be referring to the president or the adviser, so it is incorrect.

8. Modifiers: Adjectives/Adverbs & Modifying Phrases

Modifiers are words and phrases that describe nouns. Adjectives modify nouns, and adverbs modify verbs, adjectives, or other adverbs. Be on the lookout for suspicious adverb-noun and adjective-verb pairings. Also be aware that many sentences will begin with a modifying phrase and a comma. The subject after the comma must be the person or thing doing the action of the modifying phrase.

9. Word Choice: Transitions & Diction

Pay attention to transition words and phrases to make sure they reflect the author's purpose. Transitions can demonstrate continuation, contrast, or cause-and-effect. In addition, the SAT may try to fool you by using words that sounds similar to the intended words, but do not make sense in context (for example, replacing "could have" with "could of").

10. Organization and Strategy

The SAT English Writing and Language section will ask you to determine the order and focus of sentences or paragraphs. You will also be asked about adding, revising, or deleting sentences as well as how a sentence fits with the purpose, audience, and focus of a paragraph or the essay as a whole.

English Example Writing and Language Question

Technology is rapidly expanding the scope of capabilities for both professional and personal use; such is the case with smart phones. Professionals now have devices available to them capable of digital media, internet access, phone communication, multi-person scheduling and office tools for documents and presentations. Businesspeople that are often mobile may maximize the use of these critical features on smartphones. Individuals who simply enjoy the luxury of multi-function devices often use these devices for frivolous pursuits such as downloading catchy ringtones, instant messaging about the latest gossip and looking up the world record for most cans crushed on one's head during the Superbowl. This fusion of capabilities and increased availability of such devices could be a sign of a growing blend in society between work and personal life, or individuals could simply be taking a luxurious approach to their connectivity in personal lives.

Technology is rapidly expanding the scope of capabilities for both professional and personal use; such is the case with smart phones. Professionals now have devices available to them capable of digital media, internet access, phone communication, multi-person scheduling and office tools for documents and presentations. Businesspeople that are often mobile may maximize the use of these critical features on smartphones. Individuals who simply enjoy the luxury of multi-function devices often use these devices for frivolous pursuits such as downloading catchy ringtones, instant messaging about the latest gossip and looking up the world record for most cans crushed on one's head during the Superbowl. This fusion of capabilities and increased availability of such devices could be a sign of a growing blend in society between work and personal life, or individuals could simply be taking a luxurious approach to their connectivity in personal lives.

The term "frivolous" implies that the author:

A. Is fascinated by the endless capabilities on smart phones.

B. Hopes that technology ceases to expand its scope.

C. Believes that the average individual does not need a smartphone.

D. Has a smartphone.

Answer: Believes that the average individual does not need a smartphone.

Based on the contextual description of trivial uses and knowledge, "frivolous" means useless or unnecessary. So if the author believes that individuals not involved in business are unnecessarily using smartphones that the author would think that these people do not need smartphones (choice C). The author makes no mention of their specific hopes for how the technology will turn out in the future, so choice B can be eliminated. The authors matter-of-fact tone allows you to rule out "fascination" (choice A), and there is no evidence to support whether or not the author has a smartphone (choice D). Choice C is the best option.

Technology is rapidly expanding the scope of capabilities for both professional and personal use; such is the case with smart phones. Professionals now have devices available to them capable of digital media, internet access, phone communication, multi-person scheduling and office tools for documents and presentations. Businesspeople that are often mobile may maximize the use of these critical features on smartphones. Individuals who simply enjoy the luxury of multi-function devices often use these devices for frivolous pursuits such as downloading catchy ringtones, instant messaging about the latest gossip and looking up the world record for most cans crushed on one's head during the Superbowl. This fusion of capabilities and increased availability of such devices could be a sign of a growing blend in society between work and personal life, or individuals could simply be taking a luxurious approach to their connectivity in personal lives.

What is the purpose of the conclusion sentence?

    A. Draw a conclusion about what we know smartphones can do

    B. Assume where technology is headed and how it will affect society

    C. Comment on human connectivity through the use of smartphones

    D. Present two possible explanations for the growing popularity of smartphones

Answer: Present two possible explanations for the growing popularity of smartphones

The conclusion sentence states two possible paths that could explain the arrival of a growth in smartphone popularity. These two suppositions are guesses at what is causing this trend.

Because the author injects minimal bias and leaves the answer to the reader's interpretation, the author is simply presenting explanations as choice D indicates. The other choices are either irrelevant or insufficiently supported by text evidence.

English Exercise

Now try this exercise question, and see how you do.

More than Light Itself

On hot and humid summer evenings, almost everyone has witnessed fireflies, also called lightning bugs, flitting around **your yard or landing on a windowsill** (2) and occasionally emitting a soft glow. Flashing on and off like flashlights or twinkling holiday lights, a firefly is just one of the many organisms that can produce **it's** (3) own **light** (4). This feature, known as bioluminescence or cold light, **appears in nature quite often** (5).

All forms of light occur through a similar process. To understand this process, you must first know a little bit about atoms. Atoms are the **smaller** (6) parts of elements, such as iron and sodium, **which have the same chemical properties** (7). The center of an atom is called the nucleus and is composed of particles called protons and neutrons. Other particles, called electrons, orbit the nucleus of **an atom; just** (8) like the earth orbits the sun. The electrons' orbit does not change unless the electrons are excited or energized in some way. **QUESTION 9** Then, when they fall back to their normal energy level, they fall back to a lower orbit and release packets of energy called photons, **which produce light. Light from** (10) a lamp or streetlight is produced when electrons are excited by heat from electricity.

In bioluminescent organisms, electrons are excited by a chemical reaction, not heat, which is why the phenomenon is often referred to as cold light. The chemicals that various organisms use to create light are luciferin and luciferase. Luciferin is the substance that produces **light luciferase** (11) is the enzyme that causes the chemical reaction to begin. In the simplest terms, luciferase makes luciferin react with oxygen, which produces light.

QUESTION 12 1 Many organisms, **from bacteria and mushrooms to certain sea creatures, insects, and others are** (13) capable of producing their own light. 2 Certain fungi, such as the jack-o'-lantern mushroom, can also create light. 3 The orange jack-o'-lantern mushrooms are often found growing on trees in the fall. 4 Among the terrestrial creatures are fireflies, glowworms, and some centipedes and millipedes. 5 Fox fire is another type of glowing fungus, usually found growing on dead or decaying trees. 6 At night, the gills of the mushroom, found beneath the cap and partway down the stalk, emit a greenish light.

SAT English Writing and Language Exercise Questions

1. The writer is considering deleting "On hot and humid summer evenings" from the first sentence (adjusting the capitalization as needed). If the writer were to make this change, the paragraph would primarily lose:

    A. an indication of the tone that will be used in the rest of the passage.

    B. details that emphasize the time of year bioluminescence must occur.

    C. an example of the kinds of weather imperative for bioluminescence to occur.

    D. nothing, because it is irrelevant to the paragraph.

2.

    A. NO CHANGE

    B. their yard or landing on a windowsill

    C. his or her yard or landing on a windowsill

    D. your yard or landing on a windowsill

3.

    A. NO CHANGE

    B. its

    C. its'

    D. their

4. Which of the following is NOT an acceptable alternative for the bold portion?

A. light, this feature

B. light; this feature

C. light, and this feature

D. light. This dramatic feature

5. The writer would like to indicate here the surprising frequency of bioluminescence. Which choice does this most effectively while maintaining the tone of the passage and the meaning of the sentence?

   A. Actually appears in nature at a higher frequency than one might come to expect.

   B. Actually appears in nature more often than you might think.

   C. Actually appears in nature more often than it does not.

   D. Actually shows up in nature more than you could ever even believe.

6.

   A. NO CHANGE

   B. most small

   C. smallest

   D. more small

7.

   A. NO CHANGE

   B. despite having the same chemical properties as the elements.

   C. that has the same chemical properties as the elements that contain them.

   D. and have the same chemical properties as the elements that contain them.

8.

   A. NO CHANGE

B. atom just like

C. atom, just like

D. atom: just like

9. Given that all the following choices are true, which choice provides the most effective transition from the preceding sentence in the paragraph to the following one?

   A.   When electrons absorb energy, they move to a higher orbit.

   B.   When electrons take in energy, they resume their normal energy level and move to the highest orbit.

   C.   After they are energized, they move into a lower orbit.

   D.   After they are energized, they resume their normal energy level.

10. Which of the following is NOT an acceptable alternative to the bold portion?

   A. which produce light; light from

   B. which produce light. Light such as that from

   C. that produce light. Light from

   D. that produce light from

11.

   A. NO CHANGE

   B. light. Luciferase

   C. light, but luciferase

   D. light; and luciferase

12. Which of the following sentence orders makes the paragraph the most logical?

   A. NO CHANGE

   B. 1, 4, 6, 5, 2, 3

C. 1, 4, 2, 6, 5, 3

D. 1, 4, 2, 3, 6, 5

13.

A. NO CHANGE

B. from bacteria and mushrooms to certain sea creatures, insects, and others is

C. from bacteria and mushrooms to certain sea creatures and insects are

D. from bacteria, mushrooms, and certain sea creatures are

Questions 14 and 15 relate to the passage as a whole

14. The writer is considering adding a statement to the beginning of the passage, clarifying the purpose for writing. Which statement LEAST emphasizes the writer's purpose?

A. Reading this passage will inform you of instances of bioluminescence in nature and the science behind this phenomenon.

B. Although the primary cause of bioluminescence is unclear, after reading this passage, you'll know a little more about the science surrounding this magical feature of nature, a few examples of it in the wild, and the chemical reactions that cause it to occur.

C. After you finish reading this passage, you'll be able to explain scientific data about bioluminescence and provide a few examples of this wonder in the natural world around us.

D. When you've finished reading this information about bioluminescence, you'll be persuaded to study the complexities of the science behind this phenomenon, and the different forms of nature preserving themselves with a bioluminescent feature.

15. The writer would like to add a paragraph to the end of the passage challenging readers to donate money to fund research on bioluminescence in habitats around the world. Should this paragraph be added?

A. Yes, because the passage is left without a conclusion, and adding a challenge to the end of this piece is a great way to create a conclusion without repeating too much information.

B. Yes, because it would tie the whole point of the passage together while offering a way for readers to connect to the scientific data presented.

C. No, because although the passage is left without an appropriate conclusion, adding a paragraph about donating money changes the purpose of the essay.

D. No, because the paragraph that is currently at the end sums up the passage enough for the reader to be left with information about bioluminescence that he or she didn't know prior to reading.

Answers

1. Correct answer: A

Although this phrase mentions weather, the rest of the essay never indicates that bioluminescence has anything to do with the weather, which gets rid of choices B and C. D is obviously incorrect. If you completed this question second, answering all of the easy questions first and coming back to this later, you'd know that!

2. Correct answer: C

Here, the antecedent is everyone, which is singular. It requires the singular his or her, although we can all agree that you'd probably use the word their in spoken English.

3. Correct answer: B

Here, we need the possessive pronoun for firefly, so its is appropriate. It's is a contraction of it is. Its' is not a word, and their, Choice D, changes the pronoun to plural when it must be singular.

4. Correct answer: A

This one is tricky, because you have to figure out which one is NOT acceptable. Choice A creates a comma splice sentence, but every other choice is structurally sound.

5. **Correct answer: B**

Choice A is too formal, choice C is inaccurate, and Choice D is too informal. Choice B maintains the casual tone the best.

6. **Correct answer: C**

Here, the superlative form should've been used, which would make it smallest, which rules out choice A. Choices B and D are never appropriate.

7. **Correct answer: D**

This is a matter of an ambiguous pronoun reference. We're not sure if the pronoun refers back to atoms or the elements. Choice A is incorrect because it doesn't fix the ambiguity. Choice B creates a different meaning and doesn't fix the ambiguity. Choice C actually creates a new error by using the singular pronoun has.

8. **Correct answer: C**

Remember that a semicolon must follow the same rules as an end mark by joining independent clauses. Here, the second clause is not independent, so a better usage is a comma and the conjunction.

9. **Correct answer: A**

This sentence must join the previous and following sentences together. Since the following sentence mentions the lower orbit in the comparative sense, we have to assume that higher is what it's being compared to.

10. **Correct answer: D**

This is one of those NOT questions, which means you simply have to cross off the stuff that does work. Here, you're looking to form a correct sentence, so check each one by plugging in. Choice J changes the meaning of the sentences altogether, so it doesn't work.

11. **Correct answer: B**

In the passage, the sentence is a run-on. So, choice A is out. Choice C creates faulty meaning, and Choice D uses the semicolon improperly.

12. Correct answer: D

The easiest way to figure this out is by underlining the topic of each sentence, and paying close attention to transitions. That way, you'll logically figure out which should come next.

13. Correct answer: C

Choice B creates another error: subject verb agreement. Choice D leaves out some information (insects), so it has to go. Choice A is wrong because the sentence isn't parallel in context.

14. Correct answer: D

Here, you'll greatly benefit from having read the entire passage. If you skimmed, you'll miss out on what the author was clearly trying to do, which is to inform you about something. Since choice D says the author was trying to persuade you, it is wrong.

15. Correct answer: C

Although choices A and B indicate that the essay is missing a conclusion and it is, the reason for adding it is incorrect. That kind of a conclusion would neither tie anything together, nor would it keep the tone of the piece. Choice C indicates this.

SAT Math

The SAT Math is broken down into calculator and non calculator sections. The No Calculator paper is 25 mins long and you will need to answer 20 questions. The Calculator sections is 55 minutes long and consists of 38 questions. There is no guessing penalty so it is always advisable to take a guess even if you have no idea what the answer is.

A large proportion of percent of the SAT math questions will be on algebra. Make sure that you can solve systems of linear equations, factor quadratics and understand functions. Brush up on exponents and radicals as well.

Some of the questions will be on intermediate algebra and coordinate geometry. Study the equations of conic sections, quadratic formula, inequalities and intersections of the graphs of functions. It may be worth getting some math help on these if it's been some time since you covered them in high school math.

The remaining sections of the math section is geometry and trigonometry questions. Have a look at formulas for finding area, circumference and perimeter. Also know how to set up equations involving trig functions and the sides of a right triangle. This is all high school math, and you will be able to do it, but you may need to refresh.

On the calculator paper: If you don't know how to solve a problem, use your calculator to guess and check the answer choices. If the choices are numbers, plug them back into the problem to see which one works. This is a really useful tatic that helps a lot, often, not all of the options will work using this backsolving technique. If the choices are equations, plug numbers into the equations to see which one gives you an answer that makes sense according to the problem.

If you get stuck on a question, mark it and come back to it later. Spend your time wisely on the problems that are easiest for you to do. All the problems are worth the same marks so don't waste valuable time on ones you can't solve. When time is almost up, go back and fill in any bubbles you missed, even if you have to guess, remember that you are not punished for incorrect answers (other than scoring zero for it) so make sure that you guess.

SAT Math Test Question Types

Math Questions	
Math Area	**Examples**
Pre-Algebra	whole numbers, fractions, decimals, and integers; positive integer powers and square roots; ratio, proportion, and percent; multiples and factors; absolute value; one variable, linear equations; probability and counting problems; data interpretation; and mean, median, and mode
Elementary Algebra	variables, polynomials, factoring, quadratic equations, linear inequalities, integer exponents, and square roots
Intermediate Algebra	quadratic formula, radical and rational expressions, inequalities, absolute value, sequences, systems of equations, quadratic inequalities, functions, matrices, polynomial roots, and complex numbers
Coordinate Geometry	number line graphs; graphs of points, lines, polynomials, circles, and other curves; relationships between equations and graphs; slope; properties of parallel and perpendicular lines; distance formula; midpoint formula; transformations; and conics
Plane Geometry	plane figures (triangles, rectangles, parallelograms, trapezoids, circles); angles; parallel lines; perpendicular lines; translations, reflections, and rotations; 3-D geometry; perimeter, area, and volume; and logical reasoning and proofs
Trigonometry	right triangle trigonometric ratios; trigonometric functions, identities, and equations; and trigonometric functions modeling

Sample SAT Math Test Questions

To give you a better feel for the format and content of the SAT Math test, let's take a look at a few sample SAT Math questions.

Pre-Algebra Question: Mean, Median, and Mode

70, 80, 50, 20, 80, 30, 80

Seven students took an art history exam. Their scores are listed above. Which of the following statements regarding the scores is true?

I. The average (arithmetic mean) is greater than 70.

II. The mode is greater than 70.

III. The median is greater than 70.

   A. None

   B. II only

   C. I and II only

   D. II and III only

Answer: First, find the average (arithmetic mean) of the test scores. Mean = (70 + 80 + 50 + 20 + 80 + 30 + 80)/7 = 58.57. 58.57 is not greater than 70. Therefore, item I. is not true, and we can eliminate choice C.

Second, find the median of the test scores. To do so, put the test scores in ascending or descending order: 20, 30, 50, 70, 80, 80, 80. The median (the number in the middle) is 70.

Therefore, item III. is not true, and we can eliminate choice D. Third, find the mode of the test scores (the number that appears most frequently): 80. Therefore, item II. is true. Choice B is the correct answer.

Geometry Question: Plane Figures and Angles

If line m intersects the square as shown, what must the value of $x + y$ be?

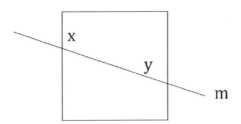

A. 45

B. 75

C. 85

D. 180

Answer: The sides of a square are parallel, so line m is a transversal to the sides of the square. That means that the angle next to (to the right of) angle y is equal to angle x by alternate interior angles. That also means that angle x is supplementary to angle y. Thus, x + y = 180. Choice D is the correct answer.

Math Hints and tips

Timing: You are given 80 minutes to answer 58 questions (over both calculator and non calculator papers). Don't think that you should allot (just over) one minute for each question. Like most math standardized tests, the difficulty range on the SAT math is relatively wide: practice answering the easier questions quickly so you'll have adequate time to answer the tougher ones.

Directions: The instructions on the math portion are relatively long and detailed. Don't waste time reading them on the day of the test. Read them before and know exactly what they will be.

Whilst the calculator and non calculator papers are different, they are very similar, a lot of the questions can be solved with or without a calculator, but you must be effective at deciding whether you do or do not on the calculator paper. My advice is to solve them all without the calculator, unless the numbers become so difficult that you cannot, this will save you a lot of time. On top of the time saved, there will be less errors, thinkof the number of typos you make when writing an email, imagine that percentage of key presses going wrong on a calculator, and the potential effects of that.

Do not continue to spend time on questions if you get stuck. Solve as many questions as you can before returning to any if time permits. Use a watch or stopwatch to make sure that you don't spend more time than is necessary on any particular question.

It's worth remembering that unless otherwise stated, you can assume:

- Figures are NOT necessarily drawn to scale.
- Geometric figures are two dimensional.
- The term line indicates a straight line.
- The term average indicates arithmetic mean.
- It's always a good idea to approach each math question using the same tatics each time.
1. Read the question

2. Look at the information provided in the question and the answer choices

3. Solve:

Back solve

Pick Numbers

Use Traditional Math

Strategically Guess

4. Check to make sure that you answered the specific question that was asked.

5. Avoid using Algebra if you can - it's often much faster to put the numbers in. I know this may not be how you were taught math in class, but this is not a standard math exam. It is a high pressure, high speed math test, so picking numbers is a good move as it speeds up your progress. This is especially helpful for number properties questions. Pick numbers that follow the rules of the question and are small and easy to work with. Avoid picking 0 or 1 because they have special properties.

6. You can backsolve when you see integers in the answer choices.

7. Translate the words in the question into math so that you can solve more easily. Take it one word or phrase at a time.

8. Recognizing number properties will save you time on test day. Number properties rules include odds and evens, prime numbers, and the order of operations.

9. Know the difference between values, ratios, and percentage. A ratio is a relationship between numbers. You need to be able to convert between percentage, fractions, and decimals very quickly.

10. You should understand key information about triangles. You must know the 30-60-90 and 45-45-90 rules.

11. Find common shapes on the SAT to help you break complex figures into simple polygons. Look in particular for triangles and squares.

12. Be on the lookout for trap answers on the SAT. Watch out for answers to steps along the way to the final answer and be careful when you see a negative sign.

Math Examples and explanations

1. Angles A and B are complementary and the measure of angle A is twice the measure of angle B. Find the measures of angles A and B.

Answer

Let A be the measure of angle A and B be the measure of angle B. Hence

$A = 2B$

Angles A and B are complementary; hence

$A + B = 90°$

But $A = 2B$; hence

$2B + B = 90$

$3B = 90$

$B = 90 / 3 = 30°$

A = 2B = 60°

2. ABCD is a parallelogram such that AB is parallel to DC and DA parallel to CB. The length of side AB is 20 cm. E is a point between A and B such that the length of AE is 3 cm. F is a point between points D and C. Find the length of DF such that the segment EF divide the parallelogram in two regions with equal areas.

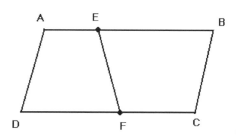

Answer

Let A1 be the area of the trapezoid AEFD. Hence

A1 = (1/2) h (AE + DF) = (1/2) h (3 + DF), h is the height of the parallelogram.

Now let A2 be the area of the trapezoid EBCF. Hence

A2 = (1/2) h (EB + FC)

We also have

EB = 20 - AE = 17, FC = 20 - DF

We now substitute EB and FC in A2 = (1/2) h (EB + FC)

A2 = (1/2) h (17 + 20 - DF) = (1/2) h (37 - DF)

For EF to divide the parallelogram into two regions of equal ares, we need to have area A1 and area A2 equal

(1/2) h (3 + DF) = (1/2) h (37 - DF)

Multiply both sides by 2 and divide thm by h to simplify to

3 + DF = 37 - DF

Solve for DF

2DF = 37 - 3

2DF = 34

DF = 17 cm

3. Find the measure of angle A in the figure below.

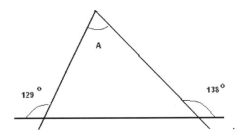

Answer

A first interior angle of the triangle is supplementary to the angle whose measure is 129° and is equal to 180 - 129 = 51°

A second interior angle of the triangle is supplementary to the angle whose measure is 138° and is equal to 180 - 138 = 42°

The sum of all three angles of the triangle is equal to 180°. Hence A + 51 + 42 = 180

A = 180 - 51 - 42 = 87°

4. ABC is a right triangle. AM is perpendicular to BC. The size of angle ABC is equal to 55 degrees. Find the size of angle MAC.

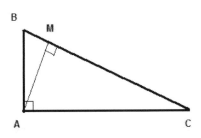

Answer

The sum of all angles in triangle ABC is equal to 180°. Hence angle ABC + angle ACM + 90° = 180°

Substitute angle ABC by 55 and solve for angle ACM angle ACM = 180 - 90 - 55 = 35°

The sum of all angles in triangle AMC is equal to 180°. Hence angle MAC + angle ACM + 90° = 180°

Substitute angle ACM by 35 and Solve for angle MAC angle MAC = 180 - 90 - angle ACM = 180 - 90 - 35 = 55°

5. Find the size of angle MBD in the figure below.

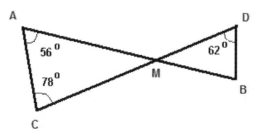

Answer

The sum of all angles in triangle AMC is equal to 180°. Hence 56 + 78 + angle AMC = 180 angle AMC = 180 - 56 - 78 = 46°

Angles AMC and DMB are vertical angles and therefore equal in measures. Hence angle DMB = 46°

The sum of angles of triangle DMB is equal to 180°. Hence angle MBD + angle DMB + 62 = 180

Substitute angle DMB by 46 and solve for angle MBD. angle MBD + 46 + 62 = 180 angle MBD = 180 - 46 - 62 = 72°

6. The size of angle AOB is equal to 132 degrees and the size of angle COD is equal to 141 degrees. Find the size of angle DOB.

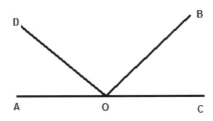

Answer

angle AOB = 132 and is also the sum of angles AOD and DOB. Hence

angle AOD + angle DOB = 132°(I)

angle COD = 141 and is also the sum of angles COB and BOD. Hence

angle COB + angle DOB = 141° (II)

We now add the left sides together and the right sides together to obtain a new equation.

angle AOD + angle DOB + angle COB + angle DOB = 132 + 141 (III)

Note that.

angle AOD + angle DOB + angle COB = 180°

Substitute angle AOD + angle DOB + angle COB in (III) by 180 and solve for angle DOB.

180 + angle DOB = 132 + 141

angle DOB = 273 - 180 = 93°

7. Find the size of angle x in the figure.

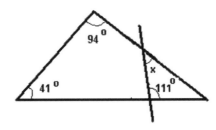

Answer

The interior angle of the quadrilateral on the left that is supplementary to x is equal to $180 - x$

The interior angle of the quadrilateral on the left that is supplementary to the angle of measure 111° is equal to 180 - 111 = 69°

The sum of all interior angles of the quadrilateral is equal to 360°. Hence 41 + 94 + 180 - x + 69 = 360

Solve for x

41 + 94 + 180 - x + 69 = 360

384 - x = 360

x = 384 - 360 = 24°

8. The rectangle below is made up of 12 congruent (same size) squares. Find the perimeter of the rectangle if the area of the rectangle is equal to 432 square cm.

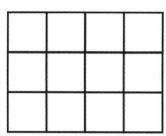

Answer

If the total area of the rectangle is 432 square cm, the area of one square is equal to =

432 / 12 = 36 square cm

Let x be the side of one small square. Hence the area of one small circle equal to 36 gives $x^2 = 36$

Solve for x

x = 6 cm

The length L of the perimeter is equal to 4x and the width W is equal to 3x. Hence L = 4 × 6 = 24 cm and W = 3 × 6 = 18 cm

The perimeter P of the rectangle is given by

P = 2 (L + W) = 2(24 + 18) = 84 cm

9. ABC is a right triangle with the size of angle ACB equal to 74 degrees. The lengths of the sides AM, MQ and QP are all equal. Find the measure of angle QPB.

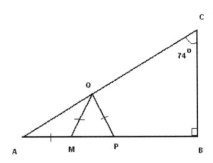

Answer

Angle CAB in the right triangle ACB is given by 90 - 74 = 16°

Sides AM and MQ in size and therefore triangle AMQ is isosceles and therefore angle AQM = angle QAM = 16°

The sum of all interior angles in triangle AMQ is equal to 180°. Hence 16 + 16 + angle AMQ = 180

Solve for angle AMQ angle AMQ = 180 - 32 = 148°

Angle QMP is supplementary to angle AMQ. Hence angle QMP = 180 - angle AMQ = 180 - 148 = 32°

Lengths of QM and QP are equal; hence triangle QMP is isosceles and therefore angle QPM is equal in size to angle QMP. Hence angle QPM = 32°

Angle QPB is supplementary to angle QPM. Hence angle QPM = 180 - angle QPM = 180 - 32 = 148°

10. Find the area of the given shape.

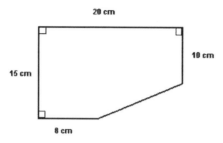

Answer

The area of the given shape may be found by subtrSATing the area of the right triangle (red) from the area of the large rectangle (see figure below).

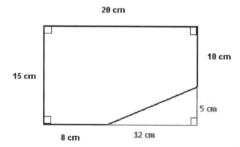

Sides of the right triangle (red) are given by 15 - 10 = 5 cm and 20 - 8 = 12 cm

Area of given shape = 20 × 15 - (1/2) × 12 × 5 = 270 cm^2

11. Find the area of the shaded region.

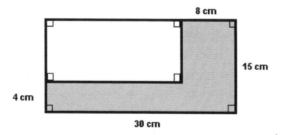

Answer

The area of the given shape may be found by subtracting the area of the rectangle at the top left from the area of the large rectangle.

Dimensions of the rectangle at top left length = 30 - 8 = 22 cm, width = 15 - 4 = 11 cm

Area of given shape = 30 × 15 - 22 × 11 = 208 cm^2

12. The vertices of the inscribed (inside) square bisect the sides of the second (outside) square. Find the ratio of the area of the outside square to the area of the inscribed square.

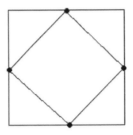

Answer

Let 2 x be the size of the side of the large square (see figure below).

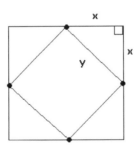

The area of the large square is (2 x) × (2x) = 4 x^2

The area of the inscribed square is y × y = y^2

Use of Pythagoras theorem gives y^2 = x^2 + x^2 = 2 x^2

Ratio R of the area of the outside square to the area of the inside square is given by $R = 4x^2 / y^2 = 4x^2 / 2x^2 = 4/2 = 2/1$

13. The art teacher at Hill Side High School is decorating her classroom by reproducing famous Art work on her walls. She has a piece that is 8 inches wide and 10 inches tall that she wants to replicate to scale on the wall. If the painting on the wall will be 6 feet tall, then approximately how wide will the painting be, in feet?

   A. 5

   B. 7

   C. 9

   D. 11

Correct Answer: A

Notice that the dimensions of the picture are given in inches, and the question asks for the dimensions of the finished painting in feet. Start by converting the dimensions of the original picture from inches to feet. To make the conversion, divide each measurement by 12. The width is 8/12 = 0.67 feet, and the height is 10/12 = 0.83 feet. Next, set up a proportion of the original measurements to the finished measurements: 0.67/0.83 = x/6. To solve for x, which is the width of the finished painting, first cross-multiply: 0.83x = (0.67)(6), or 0.83x = 4.02. Then, divide both sides by 0.83: x = 4.02 ÷ 0.83 = 4.84. The question asks for the *approximate* width of the finished painting, so round 4.84 to 5.

14. The formula for line *l* in standard form is $5x - y = 2$. Which of the following gives the formula for line *l* in slope-intercept form?

   A. $y = 5x + 2$

   B. $y = 5x - 2$

   C. $y = 2x - 5$

   D. $y = -5x - 2$

Correct Answer: B

Slope-intercept form is $y = mx + b$, where m is the slope of the line, and b is its y-intercept. To put the given equation in that form, first subtract $5x$ from both sides: $-y = -5x + 2$. Next, divide both sides by -1, making sure to divide all three terms: $y = 5x - 2$. If you picked a different answer choice, you may have made a mistake with the negatives.

15. The expression $|2-14| - |-25|$ is equal to:

    A. 41

    B.   37

    C. 13

    D. -13

Correct Answer: D

Remember order of operations on this problem. First, do the subtraction within the first absolute value sign to get $|-12| - |-25|$. Next, apply the absolute value to each term to get 12 -25, and do the subtraction: 12 -25 = -13.

16. In $\triangle JKL$ the measure of $\angle J$ is exactly 37°, and the measure of $\angle K$ is less than or equal to 63°. Which of the following phrases best describes the measure of $\angle L$?

    A. Exactly 120°

    B. Exactly 100°

    C. Exactly 80°

    D. Greater than or equal to 80°

Correct Answer: D

All the angles in a triangle add up to 180°. Because the problem gives a range of possible values for the measure of $\angle K$, plug in a number that is less than 63°, such as 60°, then solve for $\angle L$:

$$37° + 60° + \angle L = 180°$$

$$97° + \angle L = 180°$$

∠L = 83°

Only D. describes this result.

17. If 3x - 1 > 26, then which of the following is the smallest possible integer value of x ?

    A. 6

    B. 7

    C. 8

    D. 10

Correct Answer: D

First, simplify the given inequality. Start by adding 1 to both sides: 3x > 27. Next, divide both sides by 3: x > 9. Because x must be greater than 9, its smallest possible integer value is 10.

18. Paul is tying red and white ribbons around a gift box. He begins by tying the white ribbon and one red ribbon around the box. These two ribbons intersect on one face of the box at a 62° angle, as shown in the figure below. Now Paul wants to tie a second red ribbon onto the box so that the two red ribbons are parallel. What is the degree measure of the angle, indicated below, between the white ribbon and the bottom red ribbon?

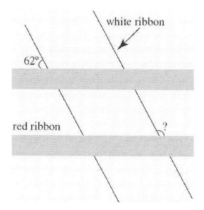

    A. 62°

    B. 76°

C. 90°

D. 118°

Correct Answer: D

This diagram of ribbons is essentially just parallel lines intersecting. The question states that the second red ribbon will be parallel to the first, and the two sides of the white ribbon are parallel to each other. The rule with intersecting parallel lines is that all big angles are equal, all small angles are equal, and any big angle plus any small angle equals 180°. The angle in question is a big angle, so to find its measurement, subtract the given small angle measurement from 180°: 180° - 62° = 118°.

19. In right triangle ΔPRS shown below, Q is the midpoint of PR. What is the length of QR, to the nearest inch?

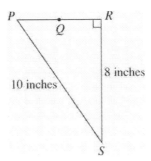

A. 2

B. 3

C. 4

D. 6

Correct Answer: B

Begin by finding the measurement of *PR*. If you recognize the side lengths of the triangle as a Pythagorean triple, you know that *PR* = 6.

Otherwise, use the Pythagorean Theorem, $a^2 + b^2 = c^2$, where *c* is the hypotenuse. Make *PR* side a:

$a^2 + 8^2 = 10^2$

$a^2 + 64 = 100$

$a^2 = 36$

$a = 6$

Since the midpoint is the exact center of a line, QR is half the length of PR: $QR = 6 \div 2 = 3$.

20. Josie notices that the textbooks for her past 3 math courses have the same length and width, but each year's textbook has more pages and weighs more than the previous year's textbook. Josie weighs the textbooks, to the nearest 0.1 ounce, for her past 3 math courses and wonders about the relationship between the number of pages in math textbooks and the weights of those textbooks. She graphs the number of pages and corresponding weights of her 3 math textbooks in the standard (x,y) coordinate plane, as shown below, and discovers a linear relationship among these 3 points. She concludes that the equation of the line that passes through these 3 points is $y = 0.1x + 2.2$.

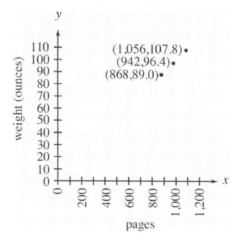

How much more, in ounces, does a math textbook with 1,056 pages weigh than one with 868 pages?

    A. 18.8

    B. 19.8

C. 54.1

D. 77.3

Correct Answer: A

The three marked points on the graph show the weight (which is the given *x*-coordinate) for books of three different lengths (the *y*-coordinate gives the number of pages). The weight of a book with 1,056 pages is 107.8 ounces, and the weight of a book with 868 pages is 89.0 ounces. To find how much more the longer book weighs, subtract the two weights: 107.8 -89 = 18.8.

21. Josie notices that the textbooks for her past 3 math courses have the same length and width, but each year's textbook has more pages and weighs more than the previous year's textbook. Josie weighs the textbooks, to the nearest 0.1 ounce, for her past 3 math courses and wonders about the relationship between the number of pages in math textbooks and the weights of those textbooks. She graphs the number of pages and corresponding weights of her 3 math textbooks in the standard (*x*,*y*) coordinate plane, as shown below, and discovers a linear relationship among these 3 points. She concludes that the equation of the line that passes through these 3 points is $y = 0.1x + 2.2$.

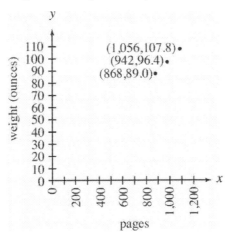

According to Josie's equation, how much would a math textbook with 1,338 pages weigh, in pounds? (Note: 16 ounces = 1 pound)

A. 7.4

B. 8.5

C. 10.2

D. 13.6

Correct Answer: B

Josie's equation, $y = 0.1x + 2.2$, is given in the description of the graph. The number of pages is shown on the x-axis of the graph, so substitute 1,338 for x in the equation: $y = 0.1(1,338) + 2.2 = 133.8 + 2.2 = 136$. This gives you the weight of the book in ounces, but the question asks for its weight in pounds. Notice that the question tells you, in the note, how many ounces are in a pound, in case you don't know. To find the weight of the book in pounds, divide its weight in ounces by 16: $136 / 16 = 8.5$.

22. All line segments that intersect in the polygon below do so at right angles. If the dimensions given are in centimeters, then what is the area of the polygon, in square centimeters?

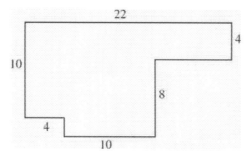

A. 168

B. 176

C. 184

D. 192

Correct Answer: D

First, divide the shape into smaller rectangles:

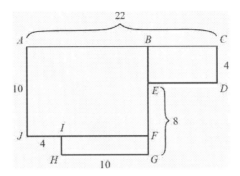

In this diagram, the points have been labeled for reference. Use the formula for the area of a rectangle, $A = lw$, to find the area of each smaller rectangle. Rectangle *BCDE* has a length of 4. To find its width, note that *AC*, which is equal to 22, will have the same measurement as *JI* + *HG* + *ED*. The measurements of two of those segments are given, so solve for *ED*:

$4 + 10 + ED = 22$

$4 + ED = 22$

$ED = 8$

The area of *BCDE* = 4 × 8 = 32. Next, find the area of *IFGH*. The width is given, but you need to find the length. *AJ* plus *IH* must equal *CD* plus *EG*, so fill in the values you know and solve for *IH*:

$10 + IH = 4 + 8$

$10 + IH = 12$

$IH = 2$

The area of *IFGH* = 2 × 10 = 20. Now find the area of *ABFJ*. Its length is given, and the width is *JI* + *IF*. Since *IF* = *HG*, the width is 4 + 10 = 14, and the area is 10 x 14 = 140. Finally, add up all the individual areas to find the area of the entire figure: 32 + 20 + 140 = 192.

23. Mr. Baylie spent 6 days grading 996 essays. He averaged 178 essays per day for the first 3 days. Which of the following is closest to his average speed, in essays graded per day, for the final 3 days?

    A. 154

B. 157

C. 160

D. 163

Correct Answer: A

To find the average speed of essay grading, divide the total essays graded by the number of days it took to grade them. This can be written as an equation, (total essays/Number of days). If Mr. Baylie averaged 178 essays per day for the first 3 days, you can find the total number of essays he graded in those three days:

$178 = $ Total $/ 3$

Total $= 178 \times 3 = 534$

In his last 3 days, he then had 996 -534 = 462 essays left to grade. Use the equation to find the average speed for the last 3 days: Average $= 462/3 = 154$.

24. For all values of y, which of the following is equivalent to $(y + 1) (y^2 - 3y + 2)$?

A. $y^3 + y^2 - y - 2$

B. $y^3 + y^2 + 2y + 2$

C. $y^3 - 2y^2 - y + 2$

D. $y^3 - 2y^2 + y - 2$

Correct Answer: C

To correctly multiply, each term in the second set of parentheses must be multiplied by both terms in the first set of parentheses. To ensure you don't miss something, write out all six terms, then combine like terms. Multiply each term in the second set of parentheses first by y, then by 1: $(y + 1)(y^2 -3y + 2) = y^3 + y^2 -3y^2 -3y + 2y + 2$. Count to be sure you have six terms before proceeding! Combine like terms to get $y^3 -2y^2 -y + 2$. If you picked another answer, you may have either forgotten a term or made a mistake with your negatives.

25. For ∠D in ΔDEF below, which of the following trigonometric expressions has value 4/5?

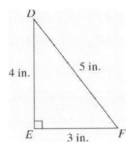

A. sin D

B. tan D

C. cos D

D. sec D

Correct Answer: C

Use *SOHCAHTOA* to solve this problem. Because 5, the number in the denominator, is the hypotenuse of the triangle, the answer to the question must be one of the trig functions that has H in the denominator (that is, sine or cosine), so you can eliminate (B) and (D). 4, the number in the numerator, is the side adjacent to ∠D. Since cos θ =adj/hyp, (c) is correct.

26. Over the weekend, Charlie bought 22 songs from an online music store. He spent a total of $17.90 on contemporary and classical songs. If contemporary songs cost $0.95 each and classical songs cost $0.75 each, then how many contemporary songs did Charlie buy? (Note: There is no sales tax charged on these songs because they were purchased online.)

    A. 7

    B. 9

    C. 10

    D. 13

Correct Answer: A

Plug In the Answers! If Charlie bought 7 contemporary songs, he must have bought 15 classical songs because he bought 22 in all. This means that Charlie spent 7($0.95) + 15($0.75) on songs altogether. These numbers add up to $17.90, which is the number we want, making A. the correct answers

SAT Reading

On the SAT Reading section, you'll meet passages, each with related questions. The passages are always about subject areas including: Literary Narrative, Social Sciences, Natural Science, and Humanities. You'll have 65 minutes to answer all 52 questions.

The English Language and Writing test and the Reading test are very different to each other and cover very different material. SAT English Writing and Language tests your knowledge of English grammar and usage conventions whereas, SAT Reading tests your reading comprehension skills.

Timing on SAT Reading

Unlike the Math section, where you take each problem as it comes, there is instead a way you should be reading passages for SAT Reading. You need to think about the time it takes to read the passages when it comes to approaching SAT Reading

It's a good idea to save most of your time for reading the passages. This feels counter-intuitive, I know, but the longer you spend on each passage, the quicker you'll be able to answer each question correctly and you'll be more accurate while you do it.

A target would be 6 minutes reading and annotating each passage, and then 3 or 4 minutes on each set of questions. Although this sounds odd, if you practice it, you will do well.

Every now and then, it is entirely plausible that you will get a question on SAT Reading that just you don't know how to do. Maybe you're reading it incorrectly; maybe there's just something about the question. With good preparation, you can reduce the risk of this happening.

Your school's English classes will have prepared you for this section, so you will be prepared.

In terms of content, SAT Reading consistently uses passages around a 10th- to 11th-grade reading level and you can the SAT will give you four passages of between 700 and 900 words.

Having a reading test on the SAT makes perfect sense. When you get to college, you'll find that you're reading *a lot*. No matter what courses you're taking, the reading load is likely to be much heavier than what you've encountered in high school.

College admissions officers have to make sure that you can cope with the reading at college. And because you'll be reading a lot—often under some time pressure—they want to see proof that you're capable of doing so.

But don't worry: even if you don't read much outside of your required schoolwork, it's not too late to start! Picking up some extracurricular reading is the best thing you can do to start boosting your SAT Reading scores. Because the SAT Reading test covers four subject areas, make sure to read in a variety of areas. General interest publications like *The New Yorker* and *The Atlantic* are very good for this kind of reading, while *The Economist* and *Scientific American* are good sources for social science and hard science reading practice, respectively.

Think about your current course load and what your homework looks like. Chances are that you're taking classes in each of the SAT Reading passage topic areas; even in classes that aren't traditionally reading-based, like chemistry, you'll still have lots of reading to do. All of this is useful help for your reading preparation.

If you're reading outside of your schoolwork, that's a positive start to your SAT Reading test preparation. However, just reading for pleasure won't help you that much, you need to take an interest in thinking critically about what you're reading whilst you're reading be thinking: What does the author think? Why did they include that example? What does that word mean in context?

Any reading you're currently doing for fun can be turned into study, as long as you treat it like an SAT passage (and that means reading it like an SAT passage).

When you start studying for SAT Reading, it can feel like every question is completely different to the rest. You can do one question then the next one is completely different.

But, if you pay attention as you work through the questions; you'll start to see a pattern emerging. Noticing these types of questions is an effective way to improve your score, because there's a particular approach that works best for solving each one.

Knowing what to expect on test day is not makes the test day much calmer, but it's also just good practice. As you encounter different types of reading passages and questions, various techniques can help you get to the right answers—if you know how to approach them.

SAT Reading Passages

The SAT Reading test is very predictable: Passages from different "genres," always in the same order. Each passage is around 700 to 900 words long and has 10 questions following the passage.

Here's what to specifically hone in on as you read each type of passage:

Literary Narrative Passages

Literary Narrative passages will include a story of events and revelation of character. You should be looking for the passage's mood or tone, the relationship of the characters, and the emotions and perspective meant by what the characters say and how they say it. Fiction passages often ask questions about how an author often uses dialogue to both describe a situation to a reader and demonstrate a character.

Social Science Passages

Social Science passages show information gathered by research. As you are reading, focus on names, dates, concepts and particular details. Pay attention to which name goes with which concept in a discussion and write down who says what. Keep an eye out for cause-effect relationships, comparisons, and sequences of events.

Humanities Passages

Passages in humanities define or examine concepts or artworks. Some passages of humanities from memoirs or personal essays may seem like fiction passages, but here they are treated as fact. Pay close attention to the speaker and perspective. A question may ask students to determine the likely response of the narrator to a hypothetical argument or circumstance. In these passages, students are asked to infer or distinguish the kinds of relationships between things, ideas, individuals, patterns or thinking styles.

Natural Science Passages

Natural Science passages usually present a science subject and explain the meaning of the topic. In a passage of natural sciences, the speaker is generally concerned with connections between natural events. As with social science passages, specific consideration should be given to cause-effect interactions, parallels, and occurrence chains. You always need to keep track of any specific laws, regulations and hypotheses as you go!

Approaching All Types of SAT Science Passages

Many non-fiction passages, notably natural science passages, will include some specific or technical language. However don't fear, the article should provide clues to the meaning of the word (if it doesn't, you'll still find a reference with a definition; it doesn't explicitly check complicated vocabulary).

As with every subject on the SAT, remember you can do the passages in any order. Some students are not fans of fiction and prefer to leave the literary narrative passage for last. Work with your preferences and strengths and complete the four passages in that order!

SAT Reading Question Types

In addition to learning how to read effectively, familiarizing yourself with the problem forms on the SAT Reading Test may help you learn how to tackle other questions, which questions you may want to bypass or save last, or which questions have certain tricks or traps. By learning how the test works, you'll get more questions right.

There are 8 basic question types on the SAT Reading test:

- Detail
- Main Idea
- Comparative Relationships
- Cause-Effect Relationships and Sequence of Events
- Inferences/Generalizations
- Meaning of Words

- Author's Voice

- Author's Method/Purpose

Here's what you need to know about each of them:

Detail Questions

Detail questions ask you to, as the name suggests find details in the passage. Most of the time, they involve nothing more than simply locating a word or phrase in the text. These are the easiest questions. The trick, though, is that SAT Reading passages are long, and detailed questions often don't give line numbers or paragraph references. As such don't get trapped in a long search of the passage as you attempt to find out tiny details.

Example: The passage states that, on average, students in 2015 applied to how many more colleges than students in 2005?

Main Idea Questions

Main idea questions ask you to determine the primary message of a paragraph, section, or an entire passage. You will see a main idea question on just about every single SAT Reading passage so you should always be prepared for one. After you finish reading the passage, summarize for yourself the main idea of the passage so you have it straight in your mind and won't be tempted by distracting answer choices that misstate what the passage says or pick up on only one part of the passage. For questions that ask you about a specific paragraph or section, remember that the first and last sentences of paragraphs are often key.

Example: The main purpose of the third paragraph is to demonstrate the author's:

Comparative Relationships

Comparative relationship questions ask you to evaluate how two or more people, viewpoints, events, theories, or so on compare. They require a higher level of thinking than the aforementioned detailed questions.

Example: According to the author, the significant difference between the director's opinion and the star actor's opinion was:

And another example: According to the passage, high school students today are different from teenagers in the past because:

Cause-Effect Relationships and Sequence of Events

Cause-effect and sequence of event questions are fairly similar, they both require you to understand what happened before something else or what happened to cause something else. They are like detailed questions in that the answer will be directly stated in the passage. The only thing you need to be careful about is realizing that the order events are discussed in the passage is not necessarily the order in which they happened.

Example: The narrator conveys that her dismissal from her first job directly resulted in:

Inferences/Generalizations

Inference and generalization questions are typically the hardest questions on the SAT because the answer won't be directly stated in the passage but will need you to take a lot of information and summarize. It is important to remember that with these questions, do not assume too much. You will only ever have to make a small leap beyond what the passage states. So if you find yourself rationalizing how an answer choice could be true, then you may have missed something. It should be more obvious.

Example: It would be reasonable to infer that the boy was not surprised by the arrival of his mother because:

Meaning of Words

Meaning of words questions are also known as word-in-context questions. You're not usually asked around complicated words here. The paragraph usually picks a term that may have multiple meanings depending on the context and asks you to pick the right one. There are two key approaches to answer these questions. First, place a blank where the word is in the passage and fill it with your own word. Then go to the answer choices and see which one best matches your choice. The other strategy is to read each answer choice back into the passage and see which one makes the most sense in the passage context (even if it doesn't make sense grammatically).

Example: As it is used in line 58, *combed* most nearly means:

Author's Voice

Author's voice questions ask you to infer how a speaker (or writer) feels about his subject. These can be difficult questions, but you should know that half of SAT Reading passages will ask you a question like this, so you should prepare for them as you read. Really hard to go back and evaluate without re-reading (which you really don't have time for). Look for clues as you read that show how an author or narrator feels about something: often these are strong adjectives, adverbs, or verbs. Sound or voice questions are often particularly important in writing.

Example: The narrator recalls her childhood in a remote area of Canada with a feeling of:

Author's Method/Purpose

Author's method or author's purpose questions challenge you to draw conclusions about what an author wants to do with a passage or why he or she has created the passage in some way. These are not incredibly common questions, but you should be prepared. The best way to prepare for these types of questions is to pay close attention to passage form when you read, and how each sentence expands on the previous one.

Example: In the context of the whole passage, the author most likely chose to include the examples of the extinction of certain bird species in order to:

Hints and Tips: SAT Reading

Now that you have seen the types of questions you are likely to see, have a look at my tips for the reading section:

Questions First

The most important things on the SAT Reading Test aren't the passages. The most important things are the questions, despite the fact they take the most time.

When you start a new passage, closely read the questions. Why? They contain the keywords you will need to discover in the passages. Underline/mark any proper nouns the questions mention and mark any line numbers mentioned in a question. These will be easy to spot later and will be good for saving time.

It's good to have a general idea of what the passage is about. Take a moment and read the first few sentences. then start searching for keywords. This is also known as skim reading. Before taking any practice tests, get to know the question types already discussed. Though the question types on the SAT Reading Test normally go from easiest to most difficult, But that's not for certain, so make sure you know all the question types.

Save the Last Question for Last

Generally, the last question will focus on the passage as a whole. So save it for the end. You will have invested a lot of information by the time you get to it and therefore will be more likely to understand it.

The SAT Reading Test (and to an equal extent the Science Test) relies on your ability to actively read. Fortunately for you, active reading on the SAT is a lot easier than it might seem at first glance.

Active reading means reading with a target in mind. This is why I suggest to look at the questions first. As you read the passage, consistently ask yourself questions: does that answer a question? How does it answer the question? Do I need more information before I mark an answer?

If you're never tried active reading, this can seem daunting, but with practice, it will become an unconscious part of your study schedule.

Timing SAT Reading

The time isn't as tough as it is on SAT Math. But, that doesn't mean it's easy. Mastering speed is the first thing you can do to make SAT Reading more manageable.

Time yourself as you practice. If you are spending more than 3 minutes reading and marking passages, you are risking not being able to finish all of the questions on test day. As you become more and more confident with your accuracy, try to get as precise as possible with the timing of your note-taking.

When you do a practice test for reading, do so with a timer. You may want to set the timer to go off every 9-10 minutes. Don't rush, but make sure you can move confidently from one passage to the next and answer all of the questions in the time you are given. Then, after 9 minutes, move on to the next passage.

Do the passages in any order, you will have 4 passages and you must always answer all 40 questions, but that doesn't mean you have to answer them in the order in which they are presented on the test. As you practice, you will start to realize which passages are easier and which are more challenging for you. But, when you do this, be extra careful to write your answers in the correct place on your answer sheet. It sounds simple, but many students have fallen foul of this.

How to Deal with "Except," "Not," or "Least" Questions on the SAT

Some of the SAT Reading passages contain test questions with words like "Except," "Not," or "Least" in them. To start, rephrase the question in easier language. Try to figure out what it's really asking. This will really help you get to the bottom of one of the trickiest types of questions on the SAT.

It is useful to determine what your job is to do, then to write it down. If a question asks, "Which of the following does NOT match the tone of the passage?" your task may be to "eliminate choices that fit the tone." This will give you a better idea of how to approach the answer choices.

Whilst questions such as this are open-ended, go back to the passage and make a prediction whenever possible. Even for a question like, "All of the following is true about Hamlet except:" you can still refer back to the passage and locate the paragraph that provides details about Hamlet.

You'll need to examine these answer choices more slowly and critically than other Reading questions. Don't rush through them. Carefully eliminate choices based on information from the passage. If you realize during the SAT Reading section that you won't have time to finish all of the questions, go to the passages with which you have had the most success in the past.

The SAT Reading Example

Stem cells have recently become an important focus for scientific research around the world. They have two important characteristics that distinguish them from other types of cells. First, they are unspecialized cells that renew themselves for long periods through cell division. Also, under certain physiologic or experimental conditions, they can be induced to become cells with special functions such as the beating cells of the heart muscle or the insulin-producing cells of the pancreas.

Scientists primarily work with two kinds of stem cells from animals and humans: embryonic stem cells and adult stem cells, which each have different functions and characteristics. Scientists discovered ways to obtain or derive stem cells from early mouse embryos more than 20 years ago. Many years of detailed study of the biology of mouse stem cells led to the discovery, in 1998, of a means to isolate stem cells from human embryos and grow the cells in the laboratory. These are called human embryonic stem cells. The embryos used in these studies were created for infertility purposes through in vitro fertilization procedures, and when they were no longer needed for that purpose, they were donated for research with the informed consent of the donor.

Stem cells are important for living organisms for many reasons. In the 3- to 5-day-old embryo, called a blastocyst, a small group of about 30 cells called the inner cell mass gives rise to the hundreds of highly specialized cells needed to make up an adult organism. In the developing fetus, stem cells in developing tissues give rise to the multiple specialized cell types that make up the heart, lung, skin, and other tissues. In some adult tissues, such as bone marrow, muscle, and brain, discrete populations of adult stem cells generate replacements for cells that are lost through normal wear and tear, injury, or disease. It has even been hypothesized that stem cells may someday become the basis for treating diseases such as Parkinson's disease, diabetes, and heart disease.

Scientists want to study stem cells in the laboratory so they can learn about their essential properties and what makes them different from specialized cell types. As scientists learn more about stem cells, it may become possible to use the cells not just in cell-based therapies but also for screening new drugs and toxins and understanding birth defects. Current research goals include both determining precisely how stem cells remain unspecialized and self-renewing for so long and identifying the signals that cause stem cells to become specialized cells.

1. The author's primary purpose in writing this passage was to

    A. argue the necessity for an effective diabetes treatment and oppose the use of mouse embryonic stem cell research

    B. aggressively defend the ethicality of gathering embryonic stem cells from human embryos

    C. hesitantly debate the role stem cells will most certainly play in future medicine

    D. explain stem cell research in relatively basic terms and point out its greatly untapped potential

Correct answer: D. The primary purpose of the passage is to introduce and describe stem cells. Additionally, the passage emphasizes the potential importance of stem cell research to our society.

2. According to the passage, the hypothesis, given in the end of the third paragraph, that stem cells hold the key to treating some of the most troublesome diseases of our time would suggest which of the following?

    A. Stem cell research will provide the means for several preventive therapies, which could be put in place in a developing fetus.

    B. Research in the field of stem cells is rapidly nearing its limit of applicability.

    C. Cells that have already become specialized are of little use when it comes to disease treatment.

    D. Stem cell research could prove more important in the medical world than anyone could have possibly anticipated.

Correct answer: D. The importance of the research is unknown, but the potential that stem cells hold may be greater than anyone can imagine based on the small amount of research that has been conducted.

3. Which one of the following statements is best supported by the properties of stem cells listed by the author?

   A. A single cell may originate as a stem cell, but it could still live the majority of its life span as a muscle tissue cell.

   B. Stem cells embody the peak of evolutionary achievement.

   C. Embryo donors are vastly decreasing in numbers as legislation is passed against these sorts of infertility procedures.

   D. Birth defects are most often caused by improper differentiation of cells from stem cells.

Correct answer: A. This answer is correct because stem cells can originate in undifferentiated form and then turn into a specific type of cell.

4. Which one of the following statements, if true, lends the most support to the author's argument that stem cell treatments will become a valuable staple in the medical world in years to come?

   A. Currently, stem cells are considered relative mysteries of science, but many researchers still believe in their promise.

   B. Stem cells multiply without any contact inhibition, much like cancer cells.

   C. Though stem cells have much potential as a new form of medical treatment, there is doubt whether we will ever be able to efficiently manipulate them.

   D. By inducing stem cells to differentiate into the tissue of choice, doctors can use healthy new cells to replace an afflicted patient's damaged or diseased cells.

Correct answer: D. If this statement were true, then stem cells could potentially cure any disease. This potential would certainly cause them to become a valuable staple of the medical community.

5. Which one of the following can replace the word essential in line 54 without significantly changing the author's intended meaning?

   A. auxiliary

   B. fundamental

   C. necessary

   D. superfluous

Correct answer: B. Scientists want to learn the basics about stem cells, which is why they want to understand their essential or fundamental properties.

6. Which one of the following best describes the organization of the passage?

   A. A topical theory is offered, the author supports the theory with mundane evidence, and then he or she concludes by calling the reader to action using emotional persuasion.

   B. Clashing hypotheses are produced, the merits of each side are debated, and then the hypotheses are merged into a single, more accurate theory.

   C. A topic is introduced, its known features and its mystery are discussed, and then future goals and applications are proposed.

   D. A scientific enigma is explained, its history is chronicled, and then certain applications are attacked for their simplicity.

Correct answer: C. The first paragraph introduces the topic of stem cells. The second and third paragraphs discuss the features and mysteries of stem cells. Finally, the fourth paragraph discusses the future goals of the research.

The SAT Reading Exercise

Directions: *Each passage is followed by several questions. After reading a passage, choose the best answer to each question and fill in the corresponding oval on your answer document. You may refer to the passages as often as necessary.*

Here they are, two North Americans, a man and a woman just over and just under forty, come to spend their lives in Mexico and already lost as they travel cross-country over the central plateau. The driver of the station wagon is Richard Everton, a blue-eyed, black-haired stubborn man. On the seat beside him is his wife, Sara. She pictures the adobe house where they intend to sleep tonight. It is a mile and a half high on the out-skirts of Ibarra, a declining village of one thousand souls. Tunneled into the mountain is the copper mine Richard's grandfather abandoned fifty years ago during the Revolution of 1910.

Dark is coming on and, unless they find a road, night trap at this desolate spot both the future operator of the Malaguefia mine and the fair-haired unsuspecting future mistress of the adobe house. Sara Everton is anticipating their arrival at a place curtained and warm, though she knows the house has neither electricity nor furniture and, least of all, kindling beside the hearth. There is some doubt about running water in the pipes. The Malaguefia mine, on the other hand, is flooded up to the second level.

"Let's stop and ask the way," says Sara. And they take a diagonal course across a cleared space of land. But the owner of this field is nowhere in sight.

"We won't get to Ibarra before dark," says Sara.

"Do you think we'll recognize the house?"

"Yes," he says, and without speaking they separately recall a faded photograph of a wide, low structure with a long veranda in front. On the veranda is a hammock, and in the hammock is Richard's grandmother, dressed in eyelet embroidery and holding a Fluted fan.

Five days ago the Evertons left San Francisco in order to extend the family's Mexican history and patch the present onto the past. To find out if there was still copper underground and how much of the rest of it was true, the width of the sky, the depth of the stars, and the air like new wine. -To weave chance and hope into a fabric that would clothe them as long as they lived.

Even their closest friends have failed to understand. "Call us when you get there," they said. "Send a telegram." But Ibarra lacks these services. "What will you do for light?" they were asked. And, "How long since someone lived in the house?" But this question collapsed of its own weight before a reply could be composed.

Every day for a month Richard has reminded Sara, "We mustn't expect too much." And each time his wife answered, "no." But the Evertons expect too much. They have experienced the terrible persuasion of a great-aunt's recollections and adopted them as their own. They have not considered that memories are like corks left out of bottles. They swell. They no longer fit.

Now here, lost in the Mexican interior, Richard and Sara remember the rock pick Richard's grandfather gave him when he was six. His grandfather had used the pick himself to chip away copper ore from extrusions that coursed like exposed arteries down the slopes of the mountains.

"What does he know about mining?" Richard's friends have asked one another. "What does she know about gasoline stoves? In case of burns, where will they find a doctor?" The friends learn that the Evertons are taking a first aid manual, antibiotics for dysentery, and a snakebite kit. There are other questions relating to symphony season tickets, Christmas, golf, sailing. To these, the answers are evasive.

A farmer, leading a burro, approaches the car from behind. He regards the two Americans. "You are not on the road to Ibarra," he says. "Permit me a moment." And he gazes first at his feet, then at the mountains, then at their luggage. "You must drive north on that dry arroyo for two kilometers and turn left when you reach a road. You will recognize it by the tire tracks of the morning bus unless rain has fallen. But this is the dry season."

"Without a tail wind we won't be bothered by the dust," says Richard, and turns north.

He is mistaken. The arroyo is smooth and soft with dust that, even in still air, spins from the car's wheels and sifts through sealed surfaces, the flooring, the dashboard, the factory-tested weather stripping. It etches black lines on their palms, sands their skin, powders their lashes, and deposits a bitter taste on their tongues.

"This must be the wrong way," says Sara, from under the sweater she has pulled over her head.

Richard says nothing. He knows it is the right way, as right as a way to Ibarra can be, as right as his decision to reopen an idle mine and bring his wife to a house built half of nostalgia and half of clay.

1. The passage is told from what point of view?

    A. First person, narrated by a minor character

    B. First person, narrated by a main character

    C. Third person, narrated by a voice outside the action of the story

    D. Third person, narrated through the perspective of one character

2. What does the passage suggest about how many, if any, preceding visits the Evertons have made to Ibarra?

    A. They have visited Ibarra before, but not for several years.

    B. They have been to Ibarra regularly to visit Richard's grandmother.

    C. They visited Ibarra once before to examine the Malaguefia mine.

    D. They have not been to Ibarra prior to this visit.

3. The main point made in the eighth paragraph is that:

    A. when everything is carefully planned, there's no risk of disappointment

    B. older relatives should not try to persuade family members to change lifestyles.

    C. people cannot live on their own memories but should instead look to the future.

    D. it's unwise to form expectations based on other people's enticing stories of another time.

4. Based on the passage, how does the house in Sara's thoughts most likely compare to the actual house where the Evertons plan to sleep?

    A. Sara's imagined house is much more inviting than the actual house.

B. Sara pictured a house that's nearly a perfect copy of the actual house.

C. The actual house is much grander than Sara is imagining.

D. The actual house is just as uninviting as the house in Sara's imagination

5. It could most reasonably be considered ironic that while Richard and Sara's copper mine:

A. is located on the side of a mountain; they get lost traveling cross-country to Ibarra.

B. was abandoned in 1910; Sara still remembers the rock pick Richard was given when he was six.

C. is located near the village of Ibarra; no one has lived in the house for several years.

D. is flooded to the second level; the house is likely to be without running water.

6. Richard thinks he and Sara will recognize the house where they intend to sleep because:

A. it's made of adobe

B. Richard's grandmother described it to them

C. they have seen an old photograph of it

D. it's the only house with a veranda

7. As it is used in paragraph 5 the phrase "the rest of it" refers to the:

A. amount of copper still left to be dug out of the mine

B. stories that Richard and Sara have heard about the natural appeal of the region.

C. town of Ibarra that Richard is anxious to find out more about

D. close friends they left behind along with their old lives in San Francisco.

8. The services mentioned specifically refer to:

A. symphony tickets and sailing excursions

B. medical aid and antibiotics.

C. electricity and running water

D. telephone calls and telegrams

9. The list "symphony season tickets, Christmas, golf, sailing" is a reference to Richard and Sara's

   A. unwillingness to spend money frivolously

   B. concerns about heading for Ibarra.

   C. recreational opportunities in Mexico

   D. former social lives in San Francisco.

10. According to the passage, the farmer tells the Evertons that it's the dry season to make the point that the:

   A. tire tracks of the bus should still be visible on the road

   B. drive to Ibarra will be hot and dusty.

   C. Evertons should reach Ibarra before it begins to rain.

   D. Evertons should have brought drinking water with them

Answers:

1. Correct Answer: C		6. Correct Answer: C
2. Correct Answer: D		7. Correct Answer: B
3. Correct Answer: D		8. Correct Answer: D
4. Correct Answer: A		9. Correct Answer: D
5. Correct Answer: D		10. Correct Answer: A

SAT Essay Prompt

The SAT Writing is optional, but a small number of colleges require or recommend that you sit it. Normally, you will have to finalize testing decisions well before you finalize their lists of where you will apply to college, so a significant majority of students still take the essay exams each year.

Despite the decline in colleges requiring an ACT or SAT essay. It is still worthwhile to do it. Some colleges requiring the essay will not super score test dates without the essay. With a minimum amount of practice, most students can reach the 25th–75th percentile score ranges of even the most elite colleges in the country. In other words, there are more positives than negatives when looking at an extended test day. All this and then if you skip the essay, then plans change, you could be scrambling to fit in an additional test date if something changes with your applications.

The rest of your SAT that you've met already is composed of the three components Reading, Writing and Language, and Math. You have 3 hours to complete these basic sections (not including breaks). The optional SAT Essay adds another 50 minutes to an already long day, but I really do recommend that you take it.

During the SAT Essay section, you'll be presented with a passage between 650 and 750 words. In the 50 minutes, you must read the passage and respond to the corresponding SAT Essay prompts. This tests your ability to analyze the author's argument in terms of the author's use of evidence, reasoning, and other rhetorical techniques.

Sharing your opinions on the passage itself or simply summarizing it will not successfully earn you a high overall score on this part of the SAT. Drawing from the passage itself, you'll need to break down the points being made in conjunction with how and why they're being made. Preparing ahead of time and walking into the test with a game plan will help you in doing just that.

Success on the SAT Essay depends on preparation as well as execution. It's vitally important that you understand the SAT Essay Scoring System. Unlike your multiple-choice answers, which are scored as either correct or incorrect, the SAT Essay is assigned three scores. Two readers will score your Essay separately and assign a score of 1 to 4 for each of three sections that include Reading, Analysis, and Writing. The two reader's scores are then added together. SAT Essay score reports provide these three separate scores, each on a 2 to 8 scale. For example, a possible score combination would be 6 Reading / 7 Analysis / 6 Writing.

Your Reading score will reflect how well your essay shows that you understood the passage. Your Analysis score will reflect how well your essay analyzes how the author went about persuading the audience. Finally, your Writing score will reflect the cohesiveness of your essay as well as how well it demonstrates a command of language and the conventions of standard written English.

My best advice is to begin with a plan. Once you've carefully read through the provided passage and corresponding prompt, take a minute to compose your thoughts in a rough outline. Mapping out your approach for an introduction, body, and conclusion when the content is fresh in your mind will ensure that you don't arrive at the end of your response with holes in your argument. An outline also helps you plan your writing by giving you a clear sense of direction when transitioning from one point to the next.

As you would for any essay written for a class in school, make sure you develop your SAT essay in a structured, connected way. In your introduction, offer a strong thesis statement that relates back to the SAT Essay prompt and make sure each element in the body of your response ties back to support it. Conclude with more than just a summary of what you've written. Consider, for example, ways you might put what you've written into a broader context or offer a memorable insight based on the analysis you've provided.

Don't forget to proofread your essay, like you were taught at school to prewrite, draft, revise, edit, and proofread work.

The stress of writing in a time crunch is enough to make anyone make mistakes. However, if they aren't fixed with proofreading they just might be what stands between you and great score on your SAT Writing. Use the final five minutes to fix errors and polish your writing if you can. Put an exclamation point where you had a period, changing that "they're" that should've been "their," or insert the word you missed.

By making these small changes, you're both making your essay easier to read and understand and showing that you're prepared for college-level writing. And that's what it's all about.

It's also important that your writing is neat and legible, people can only score what they can read.

SAT essay graders only have about a minute or two to read each essay. They won't spend ages re-reading your essay and deciding if the letters you have written are what they read them as.

If writing neatly is a challenge for you, take your time and try practicing before the test!

SAT Essay Prompt

The prompt that you will be given will say something like:

You have 50 minutes to read the passage and write an essay in response to the prompt provided inside this booklet.

After this you will be required to respond to the prompt.

The main components of the successful SAT which are:

Ideas & Analysis: A High-scoring essay should address the question that is stated and make it abundantly clear what your own perspective on this is. You must also analyze how your perspective is linked to at least one other.

Ideas and Analysis is the hardest part to really get to grips with; it's tough to do everything you need to do well at all, much less in 50 minutes. You must demonstrate that you understand as many sides of the issue as possible. You can do this by discussing those sides of the issue, why people might have those opinions, and whether those opinions are logical or not.

Development & Support: development of ideas and support for claims deepen insight and broaden context. An integrated line of skillful reasoning and illustration effectively conveys the significance of the argument. If you mention some qualifications and complications this will improve your ideas and analysis.

Development & Support is another area that can be hard for students to grasp. Essentially you need to explain every point you make. If you don't have time to explain it in two to four sentences, leave it out (unless it's the only way you can get in a comparison of your perspective with another perspective). Make sure to either explain your thinking and reasoning or use specific examples to illustrate your points.

Organization of you essay means that you need to give each idea one to two paragraphs. If a logical organization for your points occurs to you (for example, if Point 1 depends on Point 2, you'd put Point 2 first), use it. If not, just list your points, a paragraph for each one.

Language use can be the hardest area for students to improve in (particularly if English is not their native language). "Word choice is skillful and precise" does include using fancy vocabulary, but it also means not repeating yourself and using the advanced vocabulary correctly. You're better off using simple vocab correctly, than complicated vocab, incorrectly.

Using "consistently varied and clear" sentence structures doesn't just mean not starting every sentence the same way, much like with word choice (and organization), it's better to be clear than to be fancy. If you get stuck and you can't think of how to vary sentences, or come up with complex vocabulary, then don't panic, write in simple sentences and get your ideas down, then return to modify it later in the test.

Even though the SAT essay has some clear published guidelines, there are a few secrets that most students don't know and that can give you a major advantage on the test.

Such as: You do not have to have real information to back up your point, you can make it up, honestly.

This is because SAT, Inc. doesn't have the time resources to fact-check every single essay. With over a million students taking the test every year, graders only have a few minutes to put a score of 1-6 to each of the four essay scoring domains. They can't check every single fact so SAT essay scoring simplifies at and all statements are taken as truth. What is important, however, is that the evidence needs to support your thesis.

If you're short on examples to prove a point, make up something realistic-sounding perhaps say that a newspaper or politician said something. It's much better than trying to write a vague paragraph without concrete evidence.

It is also key that you write over one page, there is a strong relationship between essay length and score—the longer your essay, the better your score. In a short essay, it's difficult for you to develop your points well enough to earn a decent score.

Really, you should write a page and a half if at all possible. If you can write more than a page and a half without repeating yourself or taking away from your point, then you're doing well. SAT never really announces that you should write a page and a half, but generally this is a good yardstick.

It is most important that the introduction and ending are excellent, they are more important than the rest. SAT graders have to read a lot of essays very quickly. The fastest way for them to score an essay is to find the main argument and check the first and the last paragraphs. Think about it; if you were grading hundreds of essays, would you read all of them, in depth and taking a long time, over and over? Or would you read the first and last, get a feel for it, then skim the rest? if your introduction and conclusion paragraphs are well-written and logical, it's likely the rest of the essay will be too. By reading these, the marker can usually make a good assumption as to what the score will be. They'll scan the middle to make sure it makes sense, but they probably won't read every word as closely.

A strong SAT writing strategy includes preparing enough time to write and revise your introduction and conclusion paragraphs.

Common Mistakes

We all make mistakes, and exams are an even more likely situation in which you would. However here are some of the common mistakes that you should try and avoid.

Writing in 5 words: This sentence has five words. This sentence does as well. It does sound very dull. Don't do it like this. Change the length of sentences. If you do this, your writing will be far more interesting to read, more varied and crucially; it will hold the attention of the grader.

Forgetting to offer a counter argument. Issues are rarely one-sided. As such, the side you do not support needs to be acknowledged. This opens up a way to delve into a new point in your essay. Use an opposite viewpoint to further your argument's credibility.

Misuse of grammar: Do you know the difference between a colon and a semicolon? They're just one example. Using them correctly might score you bonus points; practice using them in your everyday writing. If you incorrectly use Grammar; you will lose marks.

People always make mistakes when using fragments. Beware of fragments. Make sure every sentence has a subject (implied or otherwise) and a verb

All writers make simple mistakes all the time. But people always forget to proofread (or choose not too). Check to make sure you've written the correct to, too, or two. The same goes for they're, their, and there. Did you accidentally combine two words because your brain was going faster than your hands? Leave a few minutes at the end to check them.

The graders don't need the same information said in five different ways. Yet a common mistake is to repeat yourself. All you need to do is make your point and continue on to the next one. Try not to needlessly fill your page just because you want your essay to appear longer.

SAT Essay Key Scoring Information

The Essay is scored separately from the rest of the SAT now since changes were made in 2016. You will receive three scores, each out of 4. However this will be done 3 times, so your final raw score will be out of 2. (4 x 3 =12, 12 x2 =24)

I've already discussed the standard format of how you should write an essay. If you do all of this will get you a good score as long as you develop your points enough.

You'll have to practice this. The perfect SAT essay is something that can be mastered, but to do it well and completely every time requires practice with a lot of sample topics. You need to learn the format of an effective essay and how to fill out a complete essay within 50 minutes.

The whole essay task (reading, analyzing, planning, and writing) must be completed in 50 minutes, getting an 4 for each in Reading, Analysis, and Writing is not at all easy (especially if you want 2 different graders to score you as 4,4,4).

You have to read the article and analyze the way the author builds her/his argument, pick out the most important components to the argument, find evidence to support your interpretation, and plan out your essay before you can even start writing.

A lot depends on how quickly you can come up with a thesis and relevant support for whatever the prompt happens to be—you might find some articles easier to read and analyze the argumentative structure of than others.

You'll need to use precise language to show mastery of English writing. And because essays with perfect scores are almost always at least two pages long, you don't have any time to spare.

If you trip up on your execution of any of these aspects, the graders might not give your SAT full marks.

However; Because the essay is so formulaic, it's always possible to get a 6 across the board. Sometimes you might find the author's argument to analyze harder than others, or sometimes you might find the article more difficult to get through, but you will always be able to impress them enough to get a good score (3 on each criteria).

No college is going to base your college admissions decision on getting those last two points on an essay you had 50 minutes to write (especially when the essay is optional). The goal, really, is to show that you can write a good standard essay in that time, and an 18 is as good at demonstrating that as a 24.

Below, I've included the criteria for a 3 and a 4 in all three domains and described the differences between the 3 and 4 score levels for Reading, Analysis, and Writing. We've marked the differences between the 3 and 4 criteria in bold.

Major Differences in scoring

Reading

For a grade 3: The response demonstrates effective comprehension of the source text. The response shows an understanding of the text's central idea(s) and important details. The response is free of substantive errors of fact and interpretation with regard to the text. The response makes appropriate use of textual evidence (quotations, paraphrases, or both), demonstrating an understanding of the source text.

For a grade 4: The response demonstrates thorough comprehension of the source text. The response shows an understanding of the text's central idea(s) and of most important details and how they interrelate, demonstrating a comprehensive understanding of the text. The response is free of errors of fact or interpretation with regard to the text. The response makes skillful use of textual evidence (quotations, paraphrases, or both), demonstrating a complete understanding of the source text.

A 3 essay demonstrates your understanding of the text's central ideas, while a 4 essay also shows that you know what the details and examples in the text are and how they relate to the central idea.

Analysis

For a grade 3: The response offers an effective analysis of the source text and demonstrates an understanding of the analytical task. The response competently evaluates the author's use of evidence, reasoning, and/or stylistic and persuasive elements, and/or feature(s) of the student's own choosing. The response contains relevant and sufficient support for claim(s) or point(s) made. The response focuses primarily on those features of the text that are most relevant to addressing the task.

For a grade 4: The response offers an insightful analysis of the source text and demonstrates a sophisticated understanding of the analytical task. The response offers a thorough, well-considered evaluation of the author's use of evidence, reasoning, and/or stylistic and persuasive elements, and/or feature(s) of the student's own choosing. The response contains relevant, sufficient, and strategically chosen support for claim(s) or point(s) made. The response focuses consistently on those features of the text that are most relevant to addressing the task.

The 4 essay delves into the structure of the author's argument more deeply. The writer not only states the techniques used in the text, but also thoroughly explains their impact on the reader. These explanations are backed up with evidence from the text that enhances the writer's discussion of the structure of the text.

Writing

For a grade 3: The response is mostly cohesive and demonstrates effective use and control of language. The response includes a central claim or implicit controlling idea. The response includes an effective introduction and conclusion. The response demonstrates a clear progression of ideas both within paragraphs and throughout the essay. The response has variety in sentence structures. The response demonstrates some precise word choice. The response maintains a formal style and objective tone. The response shows a good control of the conventions of standard written English and is free of significant errors that detract from the quality of writing.

For a grade 4: The response is cohesive and demonstrates a highly effective use and command of language. The response includes a precise central claim. The response includes a skillful introduction and conclusion. The response demonstrates a deliberate and highly effective progression of ideas both within paragraphs and throughout the essay. The response has a wide variety in sentence structures. The response demonstrates a consistent use of precise word choice. The response maintains a formal style and objective tone. The response shows a strong command of the conventions of standard written English and is free or virtually free of errors.

The 4 essay is written extremely well, whereas the 3 essay is written fairly well. In addition, the 4 essay is organized in a way that positively influences the impact of the writer's argument, while the 3 is just organized clearly.

Therefore: A perfect 4 essay:

- Is extremely clear
- Is consistent, smooth, and easy to read
- Has few errors
- Is not repetitive in content or language
- Is sufficiently detailed (using evidence from the text) to fully support the writer's thesis

- Demonstrates that you understand the text and the author's claim(s)

In other words, you need to excel in every one of these aspects to get a perfect score.

That has got to be your target, and then if you fall a little short, you will still score well. Remember not to panic about the essay section, but to train well for it and trust that you are prepared.

How to split up your timings

1. Stage 1: Planning

(Time: 8-10 minutes)

Organizing your thoughts as you write will cost you way more time than if you take the time to plan out your essay before you begin writing. Hence, you must make a plan. In the long run, this will actually save you time.

Step 1: Read the Prompt Provided, Then Choose a Position

If your perspective is a "blending" of multiple perspectives, that's also fine, as long as you make sure you compare your blended perspective to each of the perspectives it combines; otherwise, you won't fulfill the "analyze the relationship between your perspective and at least one other perspective" part of the task. Bottom line: choose the perspective you think you can support the best.

Step 2: Quickly Brainstorm Evidence and Explanations

During this step, if you find that you're able to find more convincing evidence to support a different perspective than the one you've chosen, you can always change your mind, you are of course in the planning stage. Also, you don't have to write in complete sentences, or phrase things as elegantly as you will in the actual essay, so don't worry about that.

You can find evidence:

A. Opening Paragraph of the Prompt

If you haven't already, read through the paragraph at the beginning of the essay prompt. You can appropriate some or all of the examples in it to use in your own essay.

B. Personal Experience

You can tell any story (real or not) about you or someone else you know (or make up) that supports any one of your points.

C. Statistics

Again, these can be real or made up. You could invent a research study that looked at recordings of phone calls and found >80% of people end up cursing while using automated phone menus (to support perspective one), make up statistics that show automated cashiers are able to process three times as many check-outs as human cashiers (to support perspective two) or come up with any other kind of statistics that support one of the perspectives.

D. Specifics from Sources

Use knowledge of events from history or current events to support your points. If you're not certain of the details, it's all right—the essay graders won't deduct points for factually inaccurate information. For this essay, you could use the invention of the printing press (and its effects) as an example of how mechanization can lead to "unimagined possibilities."

Step 3: Brainstorm your essay.

Put down on paper how you plan to write your essay, what are the main points you will use?

Step 4: Organize Your Essay

Now that you have the main points of your essay, it's time to organize them in a way that makes sense. Make sure to include your introduction and conclusion. Think about what will go in each paragraph. This is crucial to writing a good essay.

Stage 2: Writing

(Time: 25-28 minutes)

Once you've structured your argument, it's time to write it all down!

Step 3: Introduction Paragraph & Thesis

- Write your introduction. If you can think of an interesting first sentence that brings your thesis into a larger discussion, start with that. (If writing the introduction stumps you, just leave 10-15 lines blank at the beginning of the paper and come back to it.)

- Make sure you clearly state your thesis.

Step 4: Body Paragraphs

- When you start your first body paragraph, try to think of a first sentence that refers back to the first paragraph. Ideally, you'll start every paragraph by referring back to your thesis to create a unified argument.

- Introduce your main perspective, linking it back to the counterarguments you've made against at least one of the other perspectives.

- Present one final example in support of your perspective.

Step 5: Conclusion

- Check your time. Try to have 8 minutes left at this point.

- Come up with a quick sentence that restates your thesis to wrap up the essay.

Step 6: Revising

(Time: 2-4 minutes)

You've written out a full SAT essay. The final step is to see if you can fix any errors or improve anything else about the essay.

Let's look at the complete SAT essay example:

In the last 2-4 minutes, you want to read over your essay and try to pick up a point or two by revising. In this time, you can do a number of things.

You can, of course, correct mistakes:

You can replace dull or problematic words or phrasing with fancier words or clearer turns of phrase:

Now I suggest you read the next complete example with marking criteria and then go away and write your own SAT essay, using this guideline, see how you do!

Sample SAT Essay – Score 4,4,4

SAT essay prompt

As you read the passage below, consider how Paul Bogard uses evidence, such as facts or examples, to support claims. Reasoning to develop ideas and to connect claims and evidence. Stylistic or persuasive elements, such as word choice or appeals to emotion, to add power to the ideas expressed.

Adapted from Paul Bogard, "Let There Be Dark." ©2012 by Los Angeles Times. Originally published December 21, 2012.

At my family's cabin on a Minnesota lake, I knew woods so dark that my hands disappeared before my eyes. I knew night skies in which meteors left smoky trails across sugary spreads of stars. But now, when 8 of 10 children born in the United States will never know a sky dark enough for the Milky Way, I worry we are rapidly losing night's natural darkness before realizing its worth. This winter solstice, as we cheer the days' gradual movement back toward light, let us also remember the irreplaceable value of darkness.

All life evolved to the steady rhythm of bright days and dark nights. Today, though, when we feel the closeness of nightfall, we reach quickly for a light switch. And too little darkness, meaning too much artificial light at night, spells trouble for all.

Already the World Health Organization classifies working the night shift as a probable human carcinogen, and the American Medical Association has voiced its unanimous support for "light pollution reduction efforts and glare reduction efforts at both the national and state levels." Our bodies need darkness to produce the hormone melatonin, which keeps certain cancers from developing, and our bodies need darkness for sleep. Sleep disorders have been linked to diabetes, obesity, cardiovascular disease and depression, and recent research suggests one main cause of "short sleep" is "long light." Whether we work at night or simply take our tablets, notebooks and smartphones to bed, there isn't a place for this much artificial light in our lives.

The rest of the world depends on darkness as well, including nocturnal and crepuscular species of birds, insects, mammals, fish and reptiles. Some examples are well known—the 400 species of birds that migrate at night in North America, the sea turtles that come ashore to lay their eggs—and some are not, such as the bats that save American farmers billions in pest control and the moths that pollinate 80% of the world's flora. Ecological light pollution is like the bulldozer of the night, wrecking habitat and disrupting ecosystems several billion years in the making. Simply put, without darkness, Earth's ecology would collapse....

In today's crowded, louder, more fast-paced world, night's darkness can provide solitude, quiet and stillness, qualities increasingly in short supply. Every religious tradition has considered darkness invaluable for a soulful life, and the chance to witness the universe has inspired artists, philosophers and everyday stargazers since time began. In a world awash with electric light...how would Van Gogh have given the world his "Starry Night"? Who knows what this vision of the night sky might inspire in each of us, in our children or grandchildren?

Yet all over the world, our nights are growing brighter. In the United States and Western Europe, the amount of light in the sky increases an average of about 6% every year. Computer images of the United States at night, based on NASA photographs, show that what was a very dark country as recently as the 1950s is now nearly covered with a blanket of light. Much of this light is wasted energy, which means wasted dollars. Those of us over 35 are perhaps among the last generation to have known truly dark nights. Even the northern lake where I was lucky to spend my summers has seen its darkness diminish.

It doesn't have to be this way. Light pollution is readily within our ability to solve, using new lighting technologies and shielding existing lights. Already, many cities and towns across North America and Europe are changing to LED streetlights, which offer dramatic possibilities for controlling wasted light. Other communities are finding success with simply turning off portions of their public lighting after midnight. Even Paris, the famed "city of light," which already turns off its monument lighting after 1 a.m., will this summer start to require its shops, offices and public buildings to turn off lights after 2 a.m. Though primarily designed to save energy, such reductions in light will also go far in addressing light pollution. But we will never truly address the problem of light pollution until we become aware of the irreplaceable value and beauty of the darkness we are losing.

Write an essay in which you explain how Paul Bogard builds an argument to persuade his audience that natural darkness should be preserved. In your essay, analyze how Bogard uses one or more of the features in the directions that precede the passage (or features of your own choice) to strengthen the logic and persuasiveness of his argument. Be sure that your analysis focuses on the most relevant features of the passage. Your essay should not explain whether you agree with Bogard's claims, but rather explain how Bogard builds an argument to persuade his audience.

Student Response

In response to our world's growing reliance on artificial light, writer Paul Bogard argues that natural darkness should be preserved in his article "Let There be dark". He effectively builds his argument by using a personal anecdote, allusions to art and history, and rhetorical questions.

Bogard starts his article off by recounting a personal story – a summer spent on a Minnesota lake where there was "woods so dark that [his] hands disappeared before [his] eyes." In telling this brief anecdote, Bogard challenges the audience to remember a time where they could fully amass themselves in natural darkness void of artificial light. By drawing in his readers with a personal encounter about night darkness, the author means to establish the potential for beauty, glamour, and awe-inspiring mystery that genuine darkness can possess. He builds his argument for the preservation of natural darkness by reminiscing for his readers a first-hand encounter that proves the "irreplaceable value of darkness." This anecdote provides a baseline of sorts for readers to find credence with the author's claims.

Bogard's argument is also furthered by his use of allusion to art – Van Gogh's "Starry Night" – and modern history – Paris' reputation as "The City of Light". By first referencing "Starry Night", a painting generally considered to be undoubtedly beautiful, Bogard establishes that the natural magnificence of stars in a dark sky is definite. A world absent of excess artificial light could potentially hold the key to a grand, glorious night sky like Van Gogh's according to the writer. This urges the readers to weigh the disadvantages of our world consumed by unnatural, vapid lighting. Furthermore, Bogard's alludes to Paris as "the famed 'city of light'". He then goes on to state how Paris has taken steps to exercise more sustainable lighting practices. By doing this, Bogard creates a dichotomy between Paris' traditionally alluded-to name and the reality of what Paris is becoming – no longer "the city of light", but moreso "the city of light...before 2 AM". This furthers his line of argumentation because it shows how steps can be and are being taken to preserve natural darkness. It shows that even a city that is literally famous for being constantly lit can practically address light pollution in a manner that preserves the beauty of both the city itself and the universe as a whole.

Finally, Bogard makes subtle yet efficient use of rhetorical questioning to persuade his audience that natural darkness preservation is essential. He asks the readers to consider "what the vision of the night sky might inspire in each of us, in our children or grandchildren?" in a way that brutally plays to each of our emotions. By asking this question, Bogard draws out heartfelt ponderance from his readers about the affecting power of an untainted night sky. This rhetorical question tugs at the readers' heartstrings; while the reader may have seen an unobscured night skyline before, the possibility that their child or grandchild will never get the chance sways them to see as Bogard sees. This strategy is definitively an appeal to pathos, forcing the audience to directly face an emotionally-charged inquiry that will surely spur some kind of response. By doing this, Bogard develops his argument, adding gutthral power to the idea that the issue of maintaining natural darkness is relevant and multifaceted.

Writing as a reaction to his disappointment that artificial light has largely permeated the prescence of natural darkness, Paul Bogard argues that we must preserve true, unaffected darkness. He builds this claim by making use of a personal anecdote, allusions, and rhetorical questioning.

Scoring

This response scored a 4/4/4

Reading—4

This response demonstrates thorough comprehension of the source text through skillful use of paraphrases and direct quotations.

The writer briefly summarizes the central idea of Bogard's piece ("natural darkness should be preserved; we must preserve true, unaffected darkness"), and presents many details from the text, such as referring to the personal anecdote that opens the passage and citing Bogard's use of "Paris' reputation as "The City of Light.""

There are few long direct quotations from the source text; instead, the response succinctly and accurately captures the entirety of Bogard's argument in the writer's own words, and the writer is able to articulate how details in the source text interrelate with Bogard's central claim.

The response is also free of errors of fact or interpretation.

Overall, the response demonstrates advanced reading comprehension.

Analysis—4

This response offers an insightful analysis of the source text and demonstrates a sophisticated understanding of the analytical task.

In analyzing Bogard's use of "personal anecdote, allusions to art and history, and rhetorical questions", the writer is able to explain carefully and thoroughly how Bogard builds his argument over the course of the passage. For example, the writer offers a possible reason for why Bogard chose to open his argument with a personal anecdote, and is also able to describe the overall effect of that choice on his audience:

"In telling this brief anecdote, Bogard challenges the audience to remember a time where they could fully amass themselves in natural darkness void of artificial light. By drawing in his readers with a personal encounter...the author means to establish the potential for beauty, glamour, and awe-inspiring mystery that genuine darkness can possess.... This anecdote provides a baseline of sorts for readers to find credence with the author's claims".

The cogent chain of reasoning indicates an understanding of the overall effect of Bogard's personal narrative both in terms of its function in the passage and how it affects his audience.

This type of insightful analysis is evident throughout the response and indicates advanced analytical skill.

Writing—4

The response is cohesive and demonstrates highly effective use and command of language.

The response contains a precise central claim ("He effectively builds his argument by using personal anecdote, allusions to art and history, and rhetorical questions"), and the body paragraphs are tightly focused on those three elements of Bogard's text.

There is a clear, deliberate progression of ideas within paragraphs and throughout the response. The writer's brief introduction and conclusion are skillfully written and encapsulate the main ideas of Bogard's piece as well as the overall structure of the writer's analysis.

There is a consistent use of both precise word choice and well-chosen turns of phrase ("the natural magnificence of stars in a dark sky is definite, our world consumed by unnatural, vapid lighting, the affecting power of an untainted night sky").

Moreover, the response features a wide variety in sentence structure and many examples of sophisticated sentences ("By doing this, Bogard creates a dichotomy between Paris' traditionally alluded-to name and the reality of what Paris is becoming – no longer "the city of light", but moreso "the city of light...before 2AM"").

The response demonstrates a strong command of the conventions of written English. Overall, the response exemplifies advanced writing proficiency.

Exercises

The College Board always publish the same style of essay questions on the SAT, which is good for you. They will always take the following form:

As you read the passage below, consider how [the author] uses evidence, such as facts or examples, to support claims. Reasoning to develop ideas and to connect claims and evidence.

Stylistic or persuasive elements, such as word choice or appeals to emotion, to add power to the ideas expressed.

And after the passage, you'll see this:

Write an essay in which you explain how [the author] builds an argument to persuade [her/his] audience that [whatever the author is trying to argue for]. In your essay, analyze how [the author] uses one or more of the features listed in the box above (or features of your own choice) to strengthen the logic and persuasiveness of his argument. Be sure that your analysis focuses on the most relevant features of the passage.

Your essay should not explain whether you agree with [the author]'s claims, but rather explain how [the author] builds an argument to persuade [her/his/their] audience."

Now that you know the format, let's look an example SAT essay prompt. For the first essay, I have included the text so that you get the idea.

Adapted from former US President Jimmy Carter, Foreword to Arctic National Wildlife Refuge: Seasons of Life and Land, A Photographic Journey by Subhankar Banerjee. ©2003 by Subhankar Banerjee.

The Arctic National Wildlife Refuge stands alone as America's last truly great wilderness. This magnificent area is as vast as it is wild, from the windswept coastal plain where polar bears and caribou give birth, to the towering Brooks Range where Dall sheep cling to cliffs and wolves howl in the midnight sun.

More than a decade ago, [my wife] Rosalynn and I had the fortunate opportunity to camp and hike in these regions of the Arctic Refuge. During bright July days, we walked along ancient caribou trails and studied the brilliant mosaic of wildflowers, mosses, and lichens that hugged the tundra. There was a timeless quality about this great land. As the never-setting sun circled above the horizon, we watched muskox, those shaggy survivors of the Ice Age, lumber along braided rivers that meander toward the Beaufort Sea.

One of the most unforgettable and humbling experiences of our lives occurred on the coastal plain. We had hoped to see caribou during our trip, but to our amazement, we witnessed the migration of tens of thousands of caribou with their newborn calves. In a matter of a few minutes, the sweep of tundra before us became flooded with life, with the sounds of grunting animals and clicking hooves filling the air. The dramatic procession of the Porcupine caribou herd was a once-in-a-lifetime wildlife spectacle.

We understand firsthand why some have described this special birthplace as "America's Serengeti." Standing on the coastal plain, I was saddened to think of the tragedy that might occur if this great wilderness was consumed by a web of roads and pipelines, drilling rigs and industrial facilities. Such proposed developments would forever destroy the wilderness character of America's only Arctic Refuge and disturb countless numbers of animals that depend on this northernmost terrestrial ecosystem.

The extraordinary wilderness and wildlife values of the Arctic Refuge have long been recognized by both Republican and Democratic presidents. In 1960, President Dwight D. Eisenhower established the original 8.9 million-acre Arctic National Wildlife Range to preserve its unique wildlife, wilderness, and recreational values.

Twenty years later, I signed the Alaska National Interest Lands Conservation Act, monumental legislation that safeguarded more than 100 million acres of national parks, refuges, and forests in Alaska. This law specifically created the Arctic National Wildlife Refuge, doubled the size of the former range, and restricted development in areas that are clearly incompatible with oil exploration.

Since I left office, there have been repeated proposals to open the Arctic Refuge coastal plain to oil drilling. Those attempts have failed because of tremendous opposition by the American people, including the Gwich'in Athabascan Indians of Alaska and Canada, indigenous people whose culture has depended on the Porcupine caribou herd for thousands of years. Having visited many aboriginal peoples around the world, I can empathize with the Gwich'ins' struggle to safeguard one of their precious human rights.

We must look beyond the alleged benefits of a short-term economic gain and focus on what is really at stake. At best, the Arctic Refuge might provide 1 to 2 percent of the oil our country consumes each day. We can easily conserve more than that amount by driving more fuel-efficient vehicles. Instead of tearing open the heart of our greatest refuge, we should use our resources more wisely.

There are few places on earth as wild and free as the Arctic Refuge. It is a symbol of our national heritage, a remnant of frontier America that our first settlers once called wilderness. Little of that precious wilderness remains.

It will be a grand triumph for America if we can preserve the Arctic Refuge in its pure, untrammeled state. To leave this extraordinary land alone would be the greatest gift we could pass on to future generations.

Other essay prompts include:

"Write an essay in which you explain how Jimmy Carter builds an argument to persuade his audience that the Arctic National Wildlife Refuge should not be developed for industry."

"Write an essay in which you explain how Martin Luther King Jr. builds an argument to persuade his audience that American involvement in the Vietnam War is unjust."

"Write an essay in which you explain how Eliana Dockterman builds an argument to persuade her audience that there are benefits to early exposure to technology."

"Write an essay in which you explain how Paul Bogard builds an argument to persuade his audience that natural darkness should be preserved."

"Write an essay in which you explain how Eric Klinenberg builds an argument to persuade his audience that Americans need to greatly reduce their reliance on air-conditioning."

"Write an essay in which you explain how Christopher Hitchens builds an argument to persuade his audience that the original Parthenon sculptures should be returned to Greece.

Practice Test
Section 1: SAT Reading

General Information: 52 questions.

Timing: 65 minutes.

Directions: Read each passage and answer the questions that follow it. Some questions may have more than one answer that looks correct. In that case, pick the one that answers the question most completely and correctly. Don't assume anything that isn't stated in the passage or the questions. All the information you need to answer the questions is contained in the passage, questions, and answer choices.

Questions 1–6 refer to the following passage.

Black Apollo, by Kenneth Mannin, describes the life of Ernest Everett Just, one of the first black scientists in America. Manning recounts Just's impoverished origins in South Carolina, his adaptations to a white educational system, and hiss careers as a zoology professor at Howard University and as an embryologist at Marine Biological Laboratory. Despite countless difficulties imposed upon him by a world in which a black person was not supposed to practice science. Just became an internationally esteemed biologist. His story is one of courage determination. And dedication to science but Manning's goals are more far-reaching than to simply tell a story or describe one man's life. Alter all, though just was a brilliant biologist. He was not ultimately pivotal to the development of either science or race relations in the 20th century. The Issues brought out in his story however, are pivotal. A comprehensive appreciation of the conditions that Just faced in his daily work offers a powerful lens through which to examine the development of science and racial boundaries in America.

Manning wrote Just's story as a biography. In some respects, biography does not seem to be a promising medium for great historical work. Biographies simply tell a story. Most students receive their introductions to history in science in the worship full biographies of past scientific giants. Benjamin Franklin and Albert Einstein offer excellent examples to young students of how scientists contribute to society. Biographies are popular for children's reading lists (and bestseller lists) because they have simple subjects, can present clear moral statements and manage to teach a little history at the same time. This simplicity of form, however does not preclude the biography from being a powerful medium of historical work and social commentary.

The biography yields particular rewards for the historian of science, indeed a central reason for the discipline is to show that science is a product of social forces. This principle implies that historians and sociologists have insights on the practice of science that scientists to whom the subject would otherwise fall, are less likely to produce. Moreover, if society does influence science, then it behaves historians to explain how such an important process works. The human orientation of the biography makes it an excellent medium in which historians can do this work. Were a researcher to investigate the development of scientific theory solely by reading the accounts written of a laboratory's experiments, by looking only at the science – the researcher would likely see a science moved by apparently rational forces toward a discernible goal. But this picture is incomplete and artificial. If that researcher examines a science the through people who generated it, a richer mosaic of actors emerges. The science biography has the potential to reveal both the person through the science and the science through the person. From these perspectives, the forces of politics, emotions and economics, each of which can direct science as much as rational thought, are more easily brought to light. Black Apollo is a riveting example of what a historian can accomplish with a skillful and directed use of biography.

1. Which one of the following most accurately states the main point of the passage?

    A. Ernest Everett Just was an extremely important biologist during the 20th century, both because of his contributions to the field of embryology and because of his race.

    B. Scientists tend to ignore the social, historical, and political forces that surround all scientific research and discovery, which makes their interpretations of scientific events incomplete.

C. Biographies are a popular genre for children's books because they can tell discrete stories in an accessible fashion, incorporating scientific knowledge into a person's life and thereby making it more interesting to readers.

D. Manning's work exemplifies how biography can be a powerful tool for a historian of science, who can use the genre to explore the effects of politics, economics, and emotions on the direction of scientific development.

2. According to the passage, the main goal of the discipline called history of science is to

A. illuminate the effects of social forces on scientists in a way that scientists themselves are unlikely to do

B. explain scientific discoveries in a manner that is easily understood by non-scientists

C. write biographies of important scientific figures that portray their work against a social and political background

D. influence scientific research by identifying the most important scientific contributions in history

3. What is the primary purpose of the second paragraph?

A. to describe the many things Ernest Everett Just accomplished despite the racial prejudice he faced

B. to suggest that biography is really too simple a historical form for the historian of science to use to convey complex ideas

C. to explain why biography is both a popular historical genre and a powerful medium for explaining the significance of scientific discoveries

D. to argue against using biographies to teach children about scientific figures from the past

4. The author of the passage would be most likely to agree with which one of the following statements?

A. One of the best ways to come to an understanding of the realities of race relations and scientific development in the 20th century is to read an in-depth account of the life of one of the people who lived and worked in that world.

B. The goal of a historian of science is to glorify the accomplishments of his historical subjects, embellishing them if need be.

C. A scientific historian should pay close attention to the social and literary aspects of a scientific biography and play down the actual science, because readers can turn to scientific reports to get that information.

D. Ernest Everett Just was likely the most important black biologist, and in fact one of the most important biologists, of the 20th century.

5. According to the passage, why is Ernest Everett Just significant enough to warrant a biography?

A. Just was one of the first professional black scientists in the United States.

B. Just grew up in poverty but overcame this initial adversity to attend Howard University and then become a professional scientist.

C. Just was a biologist whose work was known and respected internationally.

D. Just's daily experiences illuminate the conditions characterized by both scientific research and racial relations during his lifetime.

6. What does the author mean by the phrase "simplicity of form" (Line 38)?

A. the simple language used by many biographical writers

B. the easy-to-read page design used by most publishers of biographies

C. a writing style that is easy for schoolchildren to read and understand

D. the straightforward organization of a biography, which follows the course of the subject's life

Questions 7–13 refer to the following passage.

Sodium lauryl sulfate (SLS) is an emulsifier and surfactant that produces lather and foam that can dissolve oil and dirt on skin and hair. SLS and another similar detergent, sodium laureth sulfate (SLES), are commonly used as foaming agents in cleaners, shampoos, and toothpaste. Both of these substances are derived from coconut oil. They make liquid and paste cleansers more effective at cleansing because they allow the cleanser to disperse more readily over the object being cleaned and make it easier to rinse the cleanser away. SLS and SLES have been used for years in numerous products sold to consumers. Other foaming agents are available, SLS and SLES have remained popular because of their low cost, effectiveness, lack of taste and odor and long history of safe use.

The use of SLS and SLES comes with a few minor risks. The substances burn human eyes, a phenomenon well known to anyone who has ever gotten a drop of shampoo in her eye. A high enough concentration of SLS will burn skin if it remains in contact with the skin for a long time, though normally this is not a problem because the products containing SLES or SLS are diluted with water and quickly washed away. SLS in toothpaste can cause diarrhea in someone who swallows a large quantity of it, but it is not known to be toxic if ingested in small quantities.

Many people have become afraid of SLS and SLES in recent years, largely as a result of widespread rumors circulated on the internet that blame SLS and SLES for causing numerous ailments in humans, including hair loss, dry skin, liver and kidney disease, blindness in children and cancer, SLS has been called one the most dangerous substances used in cosmetic products. Rumors wasn't that SLS and SLES can react with other ingredients in products to form nitrates which are potential carcinogens.

Detractors of SLS and SLES point out that these substances are used in cleansers intended for the floors of garages and bathrooms and in engine degreasers. This is true; it is also true that household and garbage cleaners are not sold for cosmetic use, come with warnings of possible skin and eye irritation and are perfectly safe to use for their intended purposes.

These internet warnings of the dangers of SLS and SLES are absurd and unsubstantiated. The US food and drug administration (FDA) has approved the use of SLS and SLES in a number of personal care products. The Occupational Safety and Health Administration (OSHA), the

International Agency for research on cancer, and the American Cancer Society have all done extensive research on SLS and SLES and concluded that they do not cause cancer.

7. Which one of the following best summarizes the main idea of the passage?

   A. A few minor risks are associated with the use of SLS and SLES, but consumers should feel safe in using products containing these substances because the FDA has approved them for use in personal care products.

   B. Manufacturers of shampoos and toothpastes include the artificial chemicals SLS and SLES in their products because they are cheap and effective surfactants, despite the known dangers associated with them.

   C. SLS and SLES are detergents that are commonly used in personal care products because they are effective and safe, despite unsubstantiated rumors to the contrary.

   D. Widespread rumors circulated on the Internet blame SLS and SLES for numerous ailments in humans, including hair loss, dry skin, liver and kidney disease, blindness in children, and cancer.

8. According to the passage, what are some of the household products that commonly contain SLS or SLES?

   A. shampoo, mouthwash, sunscreen, and hair dye

   B. shampoo, toothpaste, bathroom cleaners, and engine degreasers

   C. toothpaste, engine degreasers, engine lubricants, and garage cleaners

   D. mouthwash, facial moisturizers, and baby wipes

9. The author mentions the FDA in the last paragraph most likely to

   A. point out that the FDA has approved the use of SLS and SLES in personal care products

   B. suggest that the FDA has the best interests of consumers at heart

   C. imply that the FDA's opinion that SLS and SLES are safe for use in personal care products excuses manufacturers from testing their personal care products for safety

D. refute claims that SLS and SLES are dangerous

10. According to the passage, what are some of the widely accepted risks of SLS exposure?

    A. cancer, blindness, catarSATs, dry skin, and diarrhea

    B. burning eyes, burned skin after long exposure, liver disease, and kidney disease

    C. skin irritation, eye irritation, hair loss, and diarrhea if ingested in large quantities

    D. burning eyes, burned skin after long exposure, and diarrhea if ingested in large quantities

11. Which one of the following best describes the organization of the passage?

    A. a list of known risks of exposure to SLS and SLES; a list of unsubstantiated risks of exposure to SLS and SLES; a conclusion stating that SLS and SLES are perfectly safe

    B. a description of several common surfactants and the way in which they work; several anecdotal accounts of injuries and illnesses allegedly caused by SLS and SLES; a call for the government to ban the use of SLS and SLES in consumer care products

    C. a description of the chemical composition of SLS and SLES; a list of evidence against the use of SLS and SLES in personal care products; a proposal to manufacturers suggesting that they use only naturally occurring substances in their products

    D. a description of SLS and SLES and their uses; known risks of SLS and SLES; criticisms aimed at SLS and SLES by detractors on the Internet; evidence that SLS and SLES are safe and the rumors unfounded

12. The primary purpose of the third paragraph is:

    A. to criticize makers of personal cleansing products for including harsh chemicals in their shampoos, toothpastes, and other offerings

    B. to describe the way SLS and SLES work and explain why they are commonly used in various foaming products

C. to warn readers of the dangers associated with exposure to SLS and SLES, which include cancer, skin irritation, blindness, and kidney and liver ailments

D. to explain why some people fear SLS and SLES and to list the diseases that Internet rumors have linked to the substances

13. It can be inferred from the passage that the author would be most likely to agree with which one of the following statements?

A. It is unreasonable for people to be afraid of substances that have been deemed safe by the FDA and several other major organizations, and that have a long history of safe use, simply on the basis of unsubstantiated rumors.

B. Consumers can trust the FDA to make sure that all consumer products are safe because the FDA is funded by tax dollars and takes seriously its mission to ensure the health of American citizens.

C. The Internet is not a very reliable source of information on health topics unless that information has been posted by government agencies or major advocacy groups.

D. SLS and SLES are cheap and effective surfactants and emulsifiers, but they aren't especially safe to use in products intended for direct physical contact with human skin.

Questions 14–19 refer to the following two passages. The first is adapted from Forensic Psychology and Law, by Ronald Roesch, Patricia A. Zapf, and Stephen D. Hart (Wiley). The second is adapted from Forensic Psychology: Crime, Justice, Law, Interventions, 2nd Edition, edited by Graham Davies and Anthony Beech (Wiley).

Passage A

There are many factors that may account for mistaken eyewitness identification. Wells distinguished between system variables and estimator variables. System variables affect the accuracy of eyewitness testimony that the criminal justice system has some control over. For example, the way a question is worded or the way a lineup is constructed may impact the accuracy of eyewitness identification. In these instances, the justice system has some control over these variables. Estimator variables, on the other hand, are those that may affect the accuracy of eyewitness testimony but that the criminal justice system does not have any control over. These variables have to do with the characteristics of the eyewitness or the circumstances surrounding the event witnessed. For example, the amount of attention that an eyewitness paid to a perpetrator, how long an eyewitness viewed a perpetrator, or the lighting conditions under which a perpetrator was viewed would he examples of estimator variables since they have to do with the eyewitness or the circumstances surrounding the event. The criminal justice system does not have any control over these variables. The vast majority of the research on eyewitness identifications deals with system variables since they are under the control of the justice system and thus can be modified accordingly to improve the accuracy of eyewitness identifications and testimony. Much research has shown that asking an eyewitness misleading questions will influence his or her subsequent reports of a prior observed event. Sonic theorists contend that the misleading questions serve to alter the original memory trace. Thus, a stop sign. for example, is replaced in memory with a yield sign or an empty field is replaced in memory with a field containing a red barn. Race, gender, and age are three characteristics that have been examined to determine the extent to which they impact eyewitness accuracy. Each is an estimator variable and, there-fore, out of the control of the justice system. With respect to age; the majority of the research has examined the differences between adults and children in terms of eyewitness testimony. Research on gender differences in eyewitness identification indicates that there is no evidence that females are any better or worse than males. Similarly, there is no evidence that members of one race arc better or worse at eyewitness identification than members of another race. However, there is evidence to suggest that people are better at recognizing the faces of members of their own race than they are at recognizing the faces of members of other races.

Passage B

Human cognitive abilities are incredible. Consider the task faced by an eyewitness who is present during a street crime. The cognitive system allows the witness to transform characteristics of the light reflected towards her eyes into visual information and characteristics of perturbations in the air made by the culprit's vocal system into auditory information. The person synchronizes these sources of information (and sometimes smells, tastes, and tactile information) with a highly functional knowledge base of past experiences.

At later points in time, the witness is able to use this continually adapting knowledge base to bring that distant information into the present. The witness may even be able to travel back to the past mentally to relive the event. What Tulving called episodic memory. As amazing as these cognitive abilities are, they are not perfect. Information is forgotten and distorted, and the past century of memory research has revealed some systematic patterns for these deficits. To understand how findings from memory research can be applied to a forensic context, it is necessary to understand how memory science works. Within a criminal context, eyewitness memory is a tool that. if reliable, should be diagnostic of guilt or innocence. By this we mean that presenting eyewitness evidence should usually make guilty people seem more likely to be guilty, and innocent people seem more likely to be innocent. To be reliable, evidence does not have to always be correct but it should usually be correct.

In the US supreme court's Daubert (1993) ruling, the court argued that, for scientific evidence to be presented, there should be a known error rather, the courts do not state what the maximum error rate (or the minimum reliability) should be to allow evidence to be presented in court because this threshold would likely depend on peculiarities of an individual case.

One of the main goals for eyewitness researchers is to estimate this error rate and show how it varies by different factors. Ultimately, to estimate the reliability of any forensic tool as complex and context dependent as eye witness memory, it is necessary to understand how the system works.

If a science was trying to determine the reliability of a tool to detect, for example the explosive material from a body scan device, the scientist would have the advantage that humans created the device, so the scientist could look at the blue prints. It is more difficult to understand the human cognitive system because it is the ongoing product of ad hoc engineering, a process of trial and error called evolution.

14. The author of Passage A cites research conducted to determine how all the following affect the accuracy of an eyewitness's testimony EXCEPT:

A. the eyewitness's race

B. the eyewitness's gender

C. the types of questions the eyewitness is asked

D. the amount of time that has passed since the eyewitness experienced the event

15. Which one of the following statements is most strongly supported by both passages?

A. Eyewitness testimony is highly accurate considering the complexity of human memory.

B. Eyewitness testimony is often flawed because it is influenced by a variety of factors.

C. The human memory follows an arc pattern over one's lifetime, strengthening through adulthood and then weakening as one enters old age.

D. Little if any evidence supports the fact that males provide more accurate eyewitness testimony than females.

16. Which one of the following claims about eyewitness testimony is NOT suggested by Passage A?

A. How the lighting in a particular event affects the reliability of eyewitness identification is a variable that warrants a good amount of study.

B. The accuracy of eyewitness identification can be negatively affected by the eyewitness's race.

C. The many factors that can lead to mistaken eyewitness identification can be grouped into two main categories.

D. Much research has been done to assess how the order of a lineup may affect eyewitness identification.

17. The passages have which of the following aims in common?

A. to express the need for researchers to come up with a calculable error rate to determine whether eyewitness evidence may be admissible in court

B. to define episodic memory and explain how it may come into play in judicial proceedings

C. to identify the differences between system and estimator variables

D. to understand how memory and human cognitive abilities are affected by a variety of different factors

18. Which of the following statements most accurately characterizes a difference between the two passages?

A. Passage A discusses how misleading questions can affect the accuracy of eyewitness testimony, whereas Passage B dismisses the importance of how a witness is questioned.

B. Passage A emphasizes the importance of forensic research; Passage B is primarily concerned with the way that same research influences how system variables, such as controlling lineups, are manipulated by judicial proceedings.

C. Passage A discusses the role that race plays in greater detail than does Passage B.

D. Both passages concern improving eyewitness accuracy, but Passage A focuses on controlling variables and Passage B concentrates on understanding the science behind human recollection.

19. Each of the following is supported by one or both of the passages EXCEPT:

A. Human memory sometimes fails to recollect events exactly how they happened.

B. The cognitive system is remarkable because it is able to match sensory stimuli with previous experience.

C. Testimony based on a witness's memory ideally should provide confirmation of a culprit's guilt.

D. Lighting issues and the length of time someone witnessed an event are examples of system variables.

Questions 20–26 refer to the following passage.

Public education as it is currently known was created by a German government worried about the dangers of work uprisings that were transformed by Enlightenment and Romantic educational theories into an institution genuinely concerned with developing human minds.

Before the 1700s, Europe had no public education. Parents who wanted their children to be educated paid for private schools or private tutors. The rest of the children in Europe worked. Many of them worked alongside their parents in spinning factories, producing thread for Germany's burgeoning textile industry. The textile mill owners blatantly exploited their workers, which led to increasing levels of unrest on the part of the peasants. During the 1750s King Frederick II asked his minister of Silesia, Ernest Wilhelm von Schlabrendorff, to find a way to channel the energy of the restless peasant into something that would be less dangerous to the throne.

Schlabrendorff suggested that the king could mold a compliant citizenry if he created a system of state-run schools. These schools could teach the children of the peasantry that their lot was obtained by God, that they should not try to improve it, that the government was good to them, and that they should not question authority, along with teaching them reading, writing and arithmetic. School would be compulsory, and children who did not attend could be punished by truant officers. This would shift children's primary loyalty from their parents and families to the state. Their parents would be powerless against the truant officers and thus would be forced to send their children to school whether they wanted to or not. Aristocrats liked this idea, they liked the thought of school making peasants more docile and patriotic, and they appreciated the way state-run schools would teach children of lower social classes to accept their position in life. In 1763, Frederick gave Schlabrendorff the go ahead to start opening schools and soon every child in Silesia between the ages of 7 and 15 was attending school. These earliest of school, called Spinnschulen, combined work with education. Children took classes in the mornings and spun thread in the afternoons.

By the 1800s, the Spinnschulen had metamorphosed into full day schools with state certified teachers who taught a state approved curriculum theory, much of it influence by 19th century Romanticism that directly contradicted the principle that had led to the foundation of public schools in the 1700s Johann Bernhard Basedow use the work of Enlightenment scholars to argue that education should be a holistic pursuit, incorporating physical movement, manual training, realistic teaching and the study of nature. Freidrich Froebel invented kindergarten in the mid-1800s, creating a children's garden, based on the belief that children are naturally creative and productive, and he develop special toys designed to teach specific skills and motions. Wilhelm von Humboldt specialized ins secondary and university education theory, insisting that advanced students should pursue independent research and prizing above all three educations principle: self-government by teachers, unity of teaching and academic freedom.

20. The passage is primarily concerned with discussing which one of the following?

    A. the use of public schools to disseminate political messages, as exemplified by German public schools in the 18th and 19th centuries

    B. the exploitation of the working class by German aristocracy in the 18th century and the use of public education to justify this practice

    C. the philosophical origins of public schools in 18th century Germany and the transformation in educational thinking in the 19th century

    D. the thinking of German educational theorists and their influence on modern educational practices

21. The passage suggests which one of the following about the owners of textile mills in the 1700s?

    A. They wanted their child workers to have the benefit of an education, so they opened schools within their factories and required all young workers to attend classes.

    B. Because they could pay children less than adults, they preferred to hire young workers whenever they could.

    C. They were indifferent to the well-being and needs of their workers, caring only to maximize production and profits no matter what it cost their employees.

    D. They were all aristocrats who believed their authority was divinely ordained and that, as a result of this divinely ordained position, they had a duty to care for the less fortunate people in their communities by providing work and education for them.

22. According to the passage, how did 19th-century schools differ from 18th-century schools?

A. Eighteenth-century schools were intended to make textile mills run more efficiently by making workers become more skilled at their jobs; 19th-century schools were no longer attached to textile factories.

B. Eighteenth-century schools were concerned primarily with teaching working-class children to accept their fate and love their ruler; 19th-century schools began to focus on developing the full human potential of students.

C. Eighteenth-century schools were open only to children of the aristocracy whose parents could pay their tuition. By the 19th century, schools were open to all free of charge, but poorer students had to pay their way by working in spinning factories in the afternoons.

D. Eighteenth-century schools were designed to instill patriotic ideals in the peasantry and make them docile and compliant; 19th-century schools instead tried to develop all children into freethinkers.

23. What does the author mean by the phrase "increasing levels of unrest" in Line 15?

A. riots and other forms of violence against the owners of textile factories by peasants unhappy at their treatment

B. political speeches and demonstrations by politicians trying to earn the working-class vote

C. aggression from neighboring countries looking to invade Germany

D. religious turmoil between Catholics and Protestants

24. According to the passage, what did German aristocrats think about the idea of creating public schools?

A. They feared that educating the working classes would make them less docile and accepting of their position in life and more likely to rise up and overthrow the nobles.

B. They disliked the idea of paying taxes to support public schools and resented the king and Schlabrendorff for forcing this expense on them.

C. They appreciated Schlabrendorff's brilliance in concocting an idea that would both make the peasantry more compliant and simultaneously produce more workers for the spinning factories.

D. They liked the idea because it would make the peasantry more complacent and accepting of their fate, which would help keep the aristocracy safe in their prosperity.

25. According to the passage, what was the purpose of using truant officers to keep children in school?

A. to ensure that all children received the full education that was their right, even if their parents wished instead to keep them working at home

B. to take away the authority of parents and replace it with state power over children and citizens

C. to assist parents in making sure that their children attended school as required by catching and punishing children who failed to attend

D. to indoctrinate children and their parents with political messages designed to help the aristocracy

26. According to the passage, what did nineteenth-century educational theorists believe regarding the future of education?

A. The function of state-run schools is to instill obedience, patriotism, and docility in the working classes; wealthy children whose parents can afford to pay can have a more liberal education provided by private tutors.

B. The most important subject for children to learn is religion, which is why schools should be run by the Church and should include all aspects of worship and theology.

C. Most people cannot adequately educate their children on their own, but the state has an interest in an educated citizenry, so it is the government's job to provide public education and see that people send their children to school.

D. People learn best in an environment that respects their individuality, affords them freedom, and incorporates a variety of aspects of learning, such as physical movement, manual skills, and independent exploration.

Questions 27-32 refer to the following passage.

The stored communication portion of the Electronic Communications Privacy Act (ECPA) creates statutory privacy rights for customers of and subscribers to computer network service providers. In a broad sense, ECPA "fills in the gaps" left by the uncertain application of Fourth Amendment protections to cyberspace. To understand these gaps, consider the legal protections we have in our homes. The Fourth Amendment clearly protects our homes in the physical world: Absent special circumstances, the government must first obtain a warrant before it searches there. When we use a computer network such as the Internet, however, we do not have a physical "home." Instead, we typically have a network account consisting of a block of computer storage that is owned by a network service provider, such as America Online. If law-enforcement investigators want to obtain the contents of a network account or information about its use, they do not need to go to the user to get that information. Instead, the government can obtain the information directly from the provider.

Although the Fourth Amendment generally requires the government to obtain a warrant to search a home, it does not require the government to obtain a warrant to obtain the stored contents of a network account. Instead, the Fourth Amendment generally permits the government to issue a subpoena to a network provider that orders the provider to divulge the contents of an account. ECPA addresses this imbalance by offering network account holders a range of statutory privacy rights against access to stored account information held by network service providers.

Because ECPA is an unusually complicated statute, it is helpful when approaching the statute to understand the intent of its drafters. The structure of ECPA reflects a series of classifications that indicate the drafters' judgments about what kinds of information implicate greater or lesser privacy interests. For example, the drafters saw greater privacy interests in stored emails than in subscriber account information. Similarly, the drafters believed that computing services available "to the public" required more strict regulation than services not available to the public. (Perhaps this judgment reflects the view that providers available to the public are not likely to have close relationships with their customers, and therefore might have less incentive to protect their customers' privacy.) To protect the array of privacy interests identified by its drafters, ECPA offers varying degrees of legal protection, depending on the perceived importance of the privacy interest involved. Some information can be obtained from providers with a mere subpoena; other information requires a special court order; and still other information requires a search warrant. In general, the greater the privacy interest, the greater the privacy protection.

27. The primary purpose of the passage is to

A. qualify and explain the purpose of ECPA

B. argue that the Fourth Amendment alone is not enough protection in our age of technology

C. exalt the brilliance of the drafters of the ECPA

D. describe the difficulty of obtaining a search warrant for information in cyberspace

28. Using inferences from the passage, the author would be most likely to describe the attitudes of the public network service providers referenced in line 42 as

A. ignoble

B. impious

C. pompous

D. indifferent

29. The author argues that the ECPA is an important reinterpretation of our right to privacy because

A. subpoenas are extremely easy to obtain

B. public network service providers have very little incentive to protect their customers' rights, especially if the providers can make a profit

C. the greater the need for privacy, the more protections the ECPA tends to provide

D. as our personal information becomes more likely to be stored in a nonphysical realm, the Fourth Amendment alone has a decreasing power to protect it

30. According to the author, the Fourth Amendment had what kind of effect on cyberspace privacy rights before the ECPA?

A. momentous

B. ambiguous

C. incendiary

D. progressive

31. The author most likely mentions that "our homes [are] in the physical world" (lines 11–12) in order to

A. offer a place where there are gaps to be filled in the Fourth Amendment by the ECPA

B. remind the reader of the difference between a real home and a "cyber" home

C. explain why there is less incentive for government officials to pursue obtaining personal data from computer memory when it is far easier to get a search warrant for a physical home

D. address the contrast between the relative simplicity of protecting a physical object as opposed to the uncertain protection of computer memory

32. The passage provides support for which of the following claims?

A. The drafters of the ECPA were some of the most popular legislators in America.

B. Personal emails are legally considered more private than personal account information.

C. It is considered less important to protect privacy in computing services available "to the public" than in those that are "private."

D. In our modern age, the Fourth Amendment is outdated and could be generally disregarded without effect.

Questions 33–38 refer to the following passage.

Russia is the largest of the 15 geopolitical entities that emerged in 1991 from the Soviet Union. Covering more than 17 million square kilometers in Europe and Asia, Russia succeeded the Soviet Union as the largest country in the world. As was the case in the Soviet and tsarist eras, the center of Russia's population and economic activity is the European sector, which occupies about one-quarter of the country's territory. Vast tract s of land in Asian Russia are virtually unoccupied. Although numerous Soviet programs had attempted to populate and exploit resources in Siberia and the Arctic regions of the Russian Republic, the population of Russia's remote areas decreased in the 1990s. Thirty-nine percent of Russia's territory, but only 6% of its population, in 1996 was located east of Lake Baikal, the geographical landmark in south-central Siberia. The territorial extent of the country constitutes a major economic and political problem for Russian governments lacking the far-reaching authoritarian clout of their Soviet predecessors.

In the Soviet political system, which was self-described as a democratic federation of republics, the center of authority for almost all actions of consequence was Moscow, the capital of the Russian Republic. After the breakup of the Soviet Union in 1991, that long standing concentration of power meant that many of the other 14 republics faced independence without any experience at self-governance. For Russia, the end of the Soviet Union meant facing the world without the considerable buffer zone of Soviet republics that had protected and nurtured it in various ways since the 1920s; the change required complete reorganization of what had become a thoroughly corrupt and ineffectual socialist system.

In a history-making year, the regime of President Mikhail Gorbachev of the Soviet Union was mortally injured by an unsuccessful coup in August 1991. After all the constituent republics, including Russia, had voted for independence in the months that followed the coup, Gorbachev announced in December 1991 that the nation would cease to exist. In place of the monolithic union, there remained the Commonwealth of Independent States (CIS), a loose confederation of 11 of the former Soviet republics, which now were independent states with an indefinite mandate of mutual cooperation. By late 1991, the Communist Party of the Soviet Union (CPSU) and the Communist Party of the Russian Republic had been banned in Russia, and Boris Yeltsin, who had been elected president of the Russian Republic in June 1991, had become the leader of the new Russian Federation.

Under those circumstances, Russia has undergone an agonizing process of self-analysis and refocusing of national goals. That process, which seemingly had only begun in the mid-1990s, has been observed and commented upon with more analytic energy than any similar transformation in the history of the world. As information pours out past the ruins of the Iron Curtain, a new, more reliable portrait of Russia emerges, but substantial mystery remains.

33. Which of the following best describes the main idea of the passage?

   A. In its transition to self-governance, Russia, unlike the other 14 republics, has been shaken by controversy, political failure, and stubborn remnants of the corrupt Soviet regime.

   B. Corruption among the Communist leadership was the sole problem in Soviet politics, but in the end it was enough to dissolve the Union.

   C. Russia's strength relies on the full exploitation of its resources, and the Soviet Union's inability to tap into Siberian riches led to its downfall.

   D. Over the past several years, Russia's rapid emergence from a corrupt socialist system has required political transformations on a colossal scale.

34. Which one of the following would Russian politicians probably deem the most detrimental contributor to Russian politics before 1991?

   A. the Russian Federation

   B. Boris Yeltsin

   C. Europe

   D. Communism

35. The phrase "monolithic union" most likely refers to

A. a metaphor comparing the Soviet Union to obdurate stone

B. the massiveness and perceived indestructibility of the Soviet Union in late 1991

C. the way that the republics together comprised a single association and acted as a uniform block

D. the Soviet leaders' tradition of demonstrating their power by building huge statues that were displayed around the republics

36. The second paragraph primarily serves to

A. explain why the effects of the breakup of the Soviet Union meant that the new republics would need to entirely reconstruct their political systems and attitudes

B. offer several reasons why the 15 republics were better off in the long term as part of the Soviet Union

C. describe the short-term goals of most of the republics just after the breakup of the Soviet Union

D. blame the collapse of the Soviet Union on Communism

37. It can be inferred that most Russian citizens view Siberia as which of the following?

A. intolerably inhospitable

B. politically overwhelmed

C. unfairly exploited

D. favorably desolate

38. According to the passage, all the following are true of Russia since its emergence from the Soviet Union EXCEPT:

A. it has had to deal with the loss of control of the satellite republics that constituted its buffer zone

B. it banned Communist parties from the country

C. it has attracted the attention of many social scientists, historians, and cultural analysts

D. it has developed into a corruption-free, benevolent political entity

Questions 39–42 refer to the following passage.

Melvil Dewey developed and introduced his eponymous Dewey Decimal System for book classification and arrangement in 1876. Prior to that, libraries arranged books in order of when they were acquired. Dewey's system arranged titles into 10 classes, with 10 divisions each, with each division having 10 sections. The first set, 000, includes computer and informational volumes. The 300s group encompasses the social sciences, and the last category, the 900s, identifies history and geography. For mathematics, under the general class of 500, 516 denotes geometry, and 516.3 is specific to analytic geometries.

Though the Dewey Decimal System is still in use by many general libraries, the Library of Congress Classification is preferred by many research and academic libraries. In this system, general works fall under the class A, with yearbooks sub classified as AY and dictionaries under AG.

39. According to the passage, in the Dewey Decimal System, all books are categorized into:

A. One General Class

B. One General Class and one division

C. One general class, one division, and one section

D. One general class, Including AG

40. In the first sentence of the passage, the word "eponymous" most nearly means:

A. A Most important

B. Named after a person

C. Uniquely innovative

D. Logical and simple

41. According to the passage, prior to the Dewey Decimal System books were arranged:

A. randomly

B. By age

C. By Author

D. By date of acquisition

42. Geometery is filed under what number in the Dewey Decimal System?

    A. 500

    B. 400

    C. 300

    D. 200

Questions 43–47 refer to the following passage.

Camp Wildflower is the perfect, year-round escape for you and your family. We offer a variety of accommodations to fit every preference and budget. For families who wish to enjoy a traditional camping experience, we offer large campsites with level ground for your tent, as well as hookups to access electricity and water. Our Rustic Campsites can accommodate pop-ups, trailers, and most midsize recreational vehicles. For those who prefer to camp indoors and have the budget for a few amenities, we also offer a wide range of cabins, from our Simple Bungalows to our Luxury Cottages. Campers who stay during our off-season months (October through May) will enjoy a 20 percent discount on all accommodations. Call today to plan your family's next favorite vacation!

43. Of the following combinations of accommodations, which does the passage suggest would offer the lowest possible rate at Camp Wildflower?

    A. Simple Bungalow in March

    B. Simple Bungalow in June

    C. Rustic Campsite in September

    D. Rustic Campsite in February

44. In which months is camp wildflower closed?

    A. March

    B. February

    C. None

    D. July

45. How does the article suggest that interested parties make contact?

    A. Email

    B. Mail

    C. Telephone

    D. Upon Arrival

46. Camp wildflower is marketed primarily at

    A. Families

    B. Single Men

    C. Large Groups of Women.

    D. Scout Groups

47. What does passage imply is the most expensive form of accommodation?

    A. Luxury Cottage

    B. Rustic Campsite

    C. Simple Bungalow

    D. Wild Camping.

Question 48-52 refer to the following passage.

Chang-Rae Lee's debut and award-winning novel Native Speaker is about Henry Park, a Korean-American individual who struggles to find his place as an immigrant in a suburb of New York City.

This novel addresses the notion that as the individuals who know us best, our family, peers, and lovers are the individuals who direct our lives and end up defining us. Henry Park is confronted with this reality in the very beginning of the novel, which begins:

The day my wife left she gave me a list of who I was.

Upon separating from his wife, Park struggles with racial and ethnic identity issues due to his loneliness. Through Parks' work as an undercover operative for a private intelligence agency, the author presents the theme of espionage as metaphor for the internal divide that Park experiences as an immigrant. This dual reality creates two worlds for Park and increases his sense of uncertainty with regard to his place in society. While he constantly feels like an outsider looking in, he also feels like he belongs to neither world.

Chang-Rae Lee is also a first-generation Korean American immigrant. He immigrated to America at the early age of three. Themes of identity, race, and cultural alienation pervade his works. His interests in these themes no doubt stem from his first-hand experience as a kid growing up in a Korean household while going to an American school. Lee is also author of A Gesture Life and Aloft. The protagonists are similar in that they deal with labels placed on them based on race, color, and language. Consequently, all of these characters struggle to belong in America.

Lee's novels address differences within a nation's mix of race, religion, and history, and the necessity of assimilation between cultures. In his works and through his characters, Lee shows us both the difficulties and the subtleties of the immigrant experience in America. He urges us to consider the role of borders and to consider why the idea of opening up one's borders is so frightening. In an ever-changing world in which cultures are becoming more intermingled, the meaning of identity must be constantly redefined, especially when the security of belonging to a place is becoming increasingly elusive. As our world grows smaller with increasing technological advances, these themes in Lee's novels become even more pertinent.

48. Which of the following best describes the purpose of this passage?

    A. to inform

    B. to entertain

    C. to analyze

    D. to criticize

49. Why does the author of the passage quote the first line of the novel Native Speaker?

    A. to illustrate one of the themes in the novel

    B. to show how the book is semi-autobiographical

    C. it is the main idea of the novel

    D. to create interest in the novel

50. According to the passage, which of the following is not a main theme of Lee's novels?

    A. identity

    B. espionage

    C. immigration

    D. culture

51. Based on the passage, why do Lee's novels focus on race and cultural identity?

    A. because Lee's ancestors are Korean

    B. because Lee was born in Korea

    C. because Lee feels these issues are the biggest problem facing America

    D. because Lee immigrated to America at a young age

52. How does the author of the passage feel about the ideas presented in Lee's novels?

A. certain that all borders will eventually be eliminated so world cultures will commingle and fully assimilate

B. critical regarding the role technology has played in society and how it destroys the immigrant experience

C. excited that immigrants are easily able to redefine and establish themselves in new cultures

D. concerned about the disappearance of cultures in a rapidly expanding and mixed world

Section 2: SAT Writing and Language

General Information: *44 Questions*

Timing: *35 minutes*

Directions: *In the passages that follow, certain words and phrases are underlined and numbered. In the right-hand column, you will find alternatives for the underlined part. In most cases, you are to choose the one that best expresses the idea, makes the statement appropriate for standard written English, or is worded most consistently with the style and tone of the passage as a whole. If you think the original version is best, choose "NO CHANGE." In some cases, you will find in the right-hand column a question about the underlined part. You are to choose the best answer to the question.*

You will also find questions about a section of the passage, or about the passage as a whole. These questions do not refer to an underlined portion of the passage, but rather are identified by a number or numbers in a box.

Passage

Building the Plaza de Toros

Thousands of tourists from all over the world gather in Seville, Spain each year, two weeks after Easter Holy Week, to witness the La Real Maestranza. La Real Maestranza is part of the Seville Fair, **and the Fair (1)** originated back in 1847 **when (2)** it was originally organized as a livestock fair. Of central importance to the festival are the bullfights that **took place (3)** in the Plaza de Toros, a circular ring on Baratillo Hill.

Construction on the **stunning and beautiful (4)** Plaza de Toros first **begun in 1749 but had not completed (5)** for many years after. The inner facade of the plaza (called the Palco del Príncipe or Prince's Box) was completed in 1765, and this box consists of two **parts; the (6)** access gate through which the successful bullfighters **exited (7),** and the theater box itself, which was reserved for the exclusive use of **not only the Spanish King and Queen, but for (8)** other members of the Royal Family. **(9)**

When monarch Carlos III prohibited bullfighting celebrations in 1786, work halted, **and (10)** only one-third of the plaza **had been completed (11)** at the time. The construction of the ring was finally completed in **1881, two thirds (12)** were constructed in stone, the rest in wood.

Choosing to redo them in brick, the stone grandstands were replaced between 1914 and 1915 by architect Anival Gonzalez. (13) All the rows were reconstructed with a smoother slope. Ten to twelve rows of shaded seating were constructed as well as fourteen rows in the sun and three rows of barrier. A row of armchairs was built in the superior part of the shaded area, and **they (14)** were placed in front of the theater boxes. **(15)**

1.

    A. NO CHANGE

    B. which originated

    C. which did originate

    D. and the Fair originated

2.

    A. NO CHANGE

    B. in which

    C. after which

    D. As

3.

    A. NO CHANGE

    B. had taken place

    C. did take place

    D. take place

4.

A. NO CHANGE

B. stunning yet beautiful

C. Beautiful

D. stunning, however beautiful,

5.

A. NO CHANGE

B. was began in 1749 and was not completed

C. had begun in 1749 and had completed

D. began in 1749 but was not completed

6.

A. NO CHANGE

B. parts: the

C. parts, the

D. parts the

7.

A. NO CHANGE

B. did exit

C. are exiting

D. will exit

8.

A. NO CHANGE

B. not only the Spanish King and Queen, yet for

C. not only the Spanish King and Queen, but also for

D. not the Spanish King and Queen, but also for

9. Which of the sentences below does not belong anywhere in the second paragraph?

A. The bullring is the oldest bullring constructed entirely of stone, because most others were constructed with a combination of stone and brick.

B. The stands were constructed in two levels of seating of 5 raised rows per level and 136 Tuscan sandstone columns.

C. Seville's fair is officially known as the April Fair, but in fact, it hasn't always been celebrated entirely in April and once, it even had to be celebrated in May.

D. The Royal Box has a sloping roof covered in Arabic tiles.

10.

A. NO CHANGE

B. Nevertheless

C. Because

D. even though

11.

A. NO CHANGE

B. were completed

C. will complete

D. are completed

12.

A. NO CHANGE

B. 1881; two thirds

C. 1881, two thirds,

D. 1881—two thirds

13.

A. NO CHANGE

B. Choosing to redo them in brick, between 1914 and 1915 architect Anival Gonzalez replaced the stone grandstands.

C. Choosing to redo them in brick, architect Anival Gonzalez replaced the stone grandstands between 1914 and 1915.

D. Choosing, between 1914 and 1915, to redo them in brick, architect Anival Gonzalez replaced the stone grandstands.

14.

A. NO CHANGE

B. Those

C. these chairs

D. It

15. Which of the following sentences best completes the passage?

A. Today spectators from around the world enjoy watching this traditional Spanish sport in this world-class ring.

B. Between 1729 and 1733 Felipe V stayed in Seville and received support from the Corporation in spite of being French and the first Bourbon king of Spain.

C. More than 12,500 spectators can watch the fight between the torero and the bull in this ring.

D. During the Seville Festival, men and women dress up in their finery, ideally the traditional "traje corto" (short jacket, tight trousers and boots) for men and the "faralaes" or "trajes de flamenca" (flamenco style dress) for women.

Illinois Prairies

There are different kinds of prairies in Illinois depending on the moisture gradient and soil type. The different kinds of prairie **wildflowers, are often** (16) associated with these different moisture gradients and soil types. As an ecological habitat, grasses and herbaceous wildflowers, rather than trees and shrubs, or areas with more or less permanent water, **dominated** (17) prairies.

(18) High quality prairies are interesting and colorful places to visit during the growing season **because they demonstrate high biodiversity** (19). Black soil prairie was the dominant type of prairie in central and northern **Illinois, until** (20) it was almost totally destroyed by agricultural development during the 19th century. The landscape of such prairies is rather flat. A high-quality black soil prairie has lots of wildflowers in bloom from late spring until the middle of fall. Today, small remnants of original black soil prairie can be found in pioneer **cemeteries, or at construction sites** (21)

Gravel and dolomite prairies were never very common in Illinois, and can be found primarily in northern Illinois. Gravel and dolomite prairies can be rather flat, or slightly hilly. **Yet (22)** the original gravel and dolomite prairies have been largely destroyed by modern development. They tend to be rather dry and well drained. More recently, such prairies have been found along the gravelly ballast of railroads, where they probably did not formerly exist. (23) In this case, they are degraded and **often contain flora (24)** from Western states **(25)**

Hill prairies occur primarily along the Illinois and Mississippi **rivers, hills (26)** prairies are very dry and exposed to prevailing winds from the south or west. The wild-flowers of hill prairies are similar to those **who are found (27)** found in the drier areas of gravel and dolomite prairies.

Some species that are found in hill prairies is typical **(28)** of western areas.

Sand prairies can be **moist mesic or dry and (29)** their landscape is either flat or slightly hilly. They usually occur near current or former bodies of water. **Their vegetation is sparser that that of black soil prairies. (30)**

16.

    A. NO CHANGE

B. wildflowers are often

C. wildflowers often

D. wildflowers: often

17.

A. NO CHANGE

B. dominates

C. dominating

D. dominate

18. At this point in the opening paragraph, the writer is considering adding the following true statement: In Iowa, six different types of coneflowers sway in summer breezes. Should the writer make this addition here?

A. Yes, because it helps establish that the essay is set in the Midwest.

B. Yes, because it helps reinforce the main idea of the paragraph.

C. No, because it does not make clear whether coneflowers grow in every state.

D. No, because it distracts from the main focus of the paragraph.

19. The writer is considering deleting the underlined portion from the sentence. Should the phrase be kept or deleted?

A. Kept, because it provides supporting details that reinforce the main idea of the sentence.

B. Kept, because it establishes that prairies contain more biodiversity than any other habitat.

C. Deleted, because it has already been established earlier in the paragraph that prairies have low biodiversity.

D. Deleted, because it draws attention away from the different types of prairies.

20.

    A. NO CHANGE

    B. Illinois,

    C. Illinois: until

    D. Illinois. Until

21. Given that all choices are grammatically correct, which one best establishes that black soil prairies are difficult to find today?

    A. NO CHANGE

    B. cemeteries or along old railroads.

    C. cemeteries, state parks, and surrounding farmland.

    D. cemeteries and in many neighborhoods.

22.

    A. NO CHANGE

    B. However,

    C. Unfortunately,

    D. Accordingly,

23. The writer is considering deleting the phrase "where they probably did not formerly exist" from the preceding sentence (and placing a period after the word *railroads*). Should the phrase be kept or deleted?

    A. Kept, because the information helps to establish the rampant proliferation of gravel and dolomite prairies in Illinois.

B. Kept, because it strengthens the paragraph's focus on the unchanging landscape of prairies.

C. Deleted, because it is not relevant to the description of gravel and dolomite prairies found in Illinois.

D. Deleted, because the speculation is inconsistent with the claim made earlier in the paragraph that the prairies have been largely destroyed.

24.

A. NO CHANGE

B. and many bird species migrate to them

C. consisting of a mix of native grasses and flowers and flora

D. and are of particular interest to tourists

25. For the sake of the logic and coherence of this paragraph, Sentence 4 should be placed:

A. where it is now.

B. before Sentence 1.

C. before Sentence 3.

D. before Sentence 6.

26.

A. NO CHANGE

B. rivers. Hill

C. rivers hill

D. rivers; hill,

27.

A. NO CHANGE

B. which are finding

C. if found

D. that can be found

28.

A. NO CHANGE

B. are more typical

C. typify

D. are more usual

29.

A. NO CHANGE

B. moist mesic, or dry; and

C. moist: mesic or dry, and

D. moist, mesic, or dry, and

30. Given that all of the choices are true, which best concludes the paragraph with a colorful image that relates to the description of a sand prairie?

A. NO CHANGE

B. Vegetation includes woody shrubs, wildflowers, and native prairie grasses.

C. The spectacular vegetation includes the vibrant hues of purple spiderwort, orange butterfly weed, and yellow goldenrod.

D. More than sixty colorful species of wildflowers have been identified as being native to sand prairies.

Splat, you're out

I'm not sure whose idea it was, but around the end of ninth grade, a bunch of guys from my **class, myself included: started** (31) playing paintball. If **your not familiar, its** (32) that game where two teams run around shooting at each other with gas-powered guns that fire little pellets of brightly colored paint: **et hit with a pellet, and you're out.** (33)

The first thing I learned about paintball is that it's quite an investment. A decent gun at the time **costs** (34) about seventy-five dollars, but that wasn't the end of it. Pads aren't necessary, because getting shot in the arm or leg doesn't hurt much, but you'd be a fool to play without a facemask, throat guard, and another piece of athletic equipment specific to male players. **You'll be sufficiently sick, after your first day too, to shell out for a suit of camouflage after – the odds are – getting spotted a mile away and immediately peppered** (35) and of course, paintball means regular bike rides to the sporting-goods store to buy more ammunition and get your gas canister refilled. A bunch of protective gear is required too. **(36)**

Nowadays, there are official paintball ranges you can pay to plat on, but we just played in the woods behind Bobby's house (37). It was the only location where we could be sure not to hit any homes, cars, or innocent **bystanders, that** (38) surely would have brought our paintball days to an abrupt end. We cleared brush to make paths, and dug pits and erected walls to make two opposing forts. This was more yard work than we would have done even if our parents had paid us, but no hardship was going to stand between **the thrill** (39) of sneaking up on a friend and shooting him in the butt with exploding pellets of neon goo.

Now and then, the memories of my heroism that summer still **bring** (40) a smile to my face. There was the time I discovered a secret trail up a hillside full of pricker-bushes and picked off three guys without **their having** (41) any idea where I was. Then there was the time I snuck a giant sheet of clear plexiglass into Bobby's woods, put it up between two trees, and tauntingly danced safely behind it while opponents wasted their ammo. **Sure, it was cheating, but it was also hilarious** (42)

I guess, one by one, everyone got a girlfriend and stopped coming out to the games. After a year or two, he probably did the same. I ended up selling my gun and all my gear to a kid a couple of grades younger. **I didn't exactly remember** (43) why we stopped playing. And I'd like to believe that, even now, that same equipment is still being used by some ninth grader **he is (44)** discovering the joy of squeezing the trigger on a paintball gun and hearing his shot followed by a loud pop and a swear word from his friend echoing through the woods. **(45)**

31.

    A. NO CHANGE

    B. class, myself included started

    C. class—myself included—started

    D. class. Myself included, started

32.

    A. NO CHANGE

    B. you're not familiar, it's

    C. your not familiar, it's

    D. you're not familiar, its

33. Which of the following alternatives to the underlined portion would NOT be acceptable?

    A. getting hit with a pellet means you're out.

    B. when a player is hit, they're out.

    C. a direct hit means that a player is out.

    D. you're out once you get hit, but only until the next game.

34.

    A. NO CHANGE

    B. having cost

    C. costing

D. cost

35.

A. NO CHANGE

B. The odds are, to shell out for a suit of camouflage, you'll be sufficiently sick after your first day of getting spotted, a mile away too, and immediately peppered.

C. To shell out for a suit of camouflage after your first day, the odds are you'll be sufficiently sick of getting spotted a mile away and immediately peppered too.

D. After your first day, the odds are you'll be sufficiently sick of getting spotted a mile away and immediately peppered to shell out for a suit of camouflage too.

36. For the sake of logic and coherence, Sentence 5 should be placed:

A. where it is now.

B. before Sentence 4.

C. after Sentence 1.

D. after Sentence 2.

37. Which of the following choices best introduces the paragraph?

A. NO CHANGE

B. There weren't any official paintball ranges near us (at least, not that we knew of).

C. There were a few different guys in our crew whose houses had back woods big enough to play in.

D. What we needed now was a safe place to play.

38.

A. NO CHANGE

B. bystanders

C. bystanders, whom

D. bystanders; any such occurrence

39.

A. NO CHANGE

B. our thrill

C. us and the thrill

D. ourselves, and the thrill

40.

A. NO CHANGE

B. brings

C. brought

D. have brought

41.

A. NO CHANGE

B. having

C. him having

D. DELETE the underlined portion.

42. The author is considering deleting the underlined sentence. Should the author make this deletion?

A. Yes, because such specific information about the rules of paintball is unnecessary in this brief essay.

B. Yes, because it contradicts information presented elsewhere in the essay.

C. No, because it is a humorous way of establishing that the author and his friends did not take the game too seriously.

D. No, because it is important for the reader to know that the author is someone who once cheated at paintball.

43.

A. NO CHANGE

B. don't exactly remember

C. hadn't exactly remembered

D. wouldn't remember exactly

44.

A. NO CHANGE

B. just

C. and

D. whose

10 mins break. Part way through you will get a ten minute break. Use this time to rest before you start the no calculator section

Section 3: SAT Math No Calculator

General Information: *20 Questions*

Timing: *25 minutes*

Useful formulas

    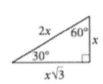

$A = \pi r^2$ $A = \ell w$ $A = \frac{1}{2}bh$ $c^2 = a^2 + b^2$ Special Right Triangles
$C = 2\pi r$

$V = \ell wh$ $V = \pi r^2 h$ $V = \frac{4}{3}\pi r^3$ $V = \frac{1}{3}\pi r^2 h$ $V = \frac{1}{3}\ell wh$

The number of degrees of arc in a circle is 360.
The number of radians of arc in a circle is 2π.
The sum of the measures in degrees of the angles of a triangle is 180.

1. $\dfrac{(4^{13} - 4^{12})}{4^{11}}$

   A. 0

   B. 1

   C. 4

   D. 12

$$\frac{13!}{}$$

2. If 2^x is an integer, which of the following represents all possible values of x ?

   A. $0 \le x \le 10$

   B. $0 < x < 9$

   C. $0 \le x < 10$

   D. $1 \le x \le 10$

3. $4a^2 - 4b^2$ is equivalent to which of the following?

   A. $(2a - 2b)(2a - 2b)$

   B. $(4a - 4b)(4a - 4b)$

   C. $(2a + 2b)(2a - 2b)$

   D. $(2a + 2b)(a - b)$

4. If $16 + 4x$ is 10 more than 14, what is the value of $8x$?

   A. 2

   B. 6

   C. 16

   D. 80

5. On Tuesday, a salesman made four sales. On the first three sales, the salesman received a commission of $2,100, $1,500, and $1,800. If the salesman's average commission for all four sales was $2,000, what was the salesman's commission on the fourth sale?

   A. $2,100

   B. $2,300

   C. $2,400

   D. $2,600

6. If $2a < 6$, and $3b > 27$, then $b - a$ can equal all of the following but not which value?

   A. 6

   B. 7

   C. 8

   D. 9

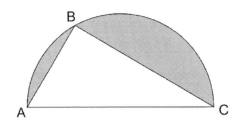

7. Triangle ABC is inscribed in the semicircle above. If the length of side *AB* is 10, and the length of side *BC* is 24, what is the area of the shaded region?

   A. 169π

   B. 84.5π

   C. $169\pi - 120$

   D. $84.5\pi - 120$

8. An asteroid travels through space at a constant rate of 2.6 million feet per day. If the distance between the asteroid and a certain planet is 10.2 million feet, approximately how many seconds will it take the asteroid to reach the planet?

   A. 80,000

   B. 120,000

   C. 350,000

   D. 250,000

9. If x and y are unique nonzero integers such that x + y = 0, then one of the below is untrue, which one is it?

   A. $|x| = |y|$

B. $x < y$

C. $xy > 0$

D. $x^2 + y^2 = 0$

10. A survey of voter preferences showed that, rounded to the nearest tenths digit, 14.2% of voters expressed a preference for an independent candidate. If 80,000 voters responded to this survey, which of the following could equal the number of voters who expressed a preference for an independent candidate? (Indicate all that apply.)

A. 11,315

B. 11,321

C. 11,390

D. 11,399

Questions 11 through 14 refer to the following graph.

Figure 1- SUBSCRIPTIONS TO NEWSMAGAZINE x, 1970–1985

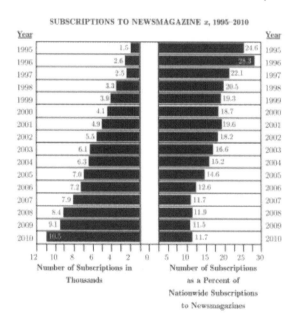

Note: Drawn to scale

NATIONWIDE NEWSMAGAZINE SUBSCRITIONS: 1972 TO 1984

Newsmagazine	1972	1975	1978	1981	1984
X	2,500	4,100	6,100	7,200	9,100
y	1,700	3,100	4,600	5,700	7,200
z	3,600	5,800	7,600	9,400	11,400
Others	3,500	8,900	18,500	34,700	51,300

11. What was the total number of subscriptions for Newsmagazine x during the year in which Newsmagazine x accounted for 14.6 percent of nationwide news magazine subscriptions?

   A. 1,020

   B. 1,980

   C. 6,300

   D. 7,000

12. In which of the following years did subscriptions to Newsmagazine *z* account for approximately 1/6 of the total nationwide magazine subscriptions?

   A. 1984

   B. 1981

   C. 1978

   D. 1975

13. What was the approximate percent increase in nationwide subscriptions to news magazines between 1970 and 1971?

   A. 4%

   B. 11%

   C. 26%

D. 51%

14. In 1973, what was the approximate number of subscriptions to newsmagazines nationwide?

A. 3,000

B. 13,000

C. 16,000

D. 20,000

Questions 15 through 17 refer to the following table.

Majors at University *X* Percentage Change in Student

Major	2015	2017
Biology	−12	8
Psychology	−10	10
Mathematics	6	11
English	−3	−10
Philosophy	11	−3

15. If 1,000 students majored in Philosophy in 2015, how many students majored in Philosophy in 2017?

A. 1,060

B. 1,077

C. 1,073

D. 1,078

16. If 1,000 students majored in Physcology and math in 2015, which of the following are the number of students who majored in physcology and math in 2017?

A. 990

B. 1176

C. 1,073

D. 1,078

The following questions are numberical answer questions. You need to write down the correct answer. In the exam you will need to fill in your bubble sheet with the numerical answer.

17. If the number of students who majored in Biology in 2015 was double the number of students who majored in English in 2015, then the number of students who majored in Biology in 2017 was what percent greater than the number of students who majored in English in 2017? Round your answer to the nearest integer.

18. The population of State X is double that of State Y. If the population concentration (people per square mile) of State X is triple that of State Y, then what is the ratio of the area of State X to the area of State Y?

19. If each of the sides of a certain square is doubled in length, by what factor will the area of the square increase?

20. Oceans, seas, and bays represent about 96.5% of Earth's water, including the water found in our atmosphere. If the volume of the water contained in oceans, seas, and bays is about 321,000,000 cubic miles, what is the approximate volume, in cubic miles, of all the world's water?

5 mins break, at this stage you will get a 5 minute break. Use this time to rest before you start the calculator section.

Section 4: SAT Math Calculator

General Information: *38 questions*

Timing: *55 minutes*

Useful formulas

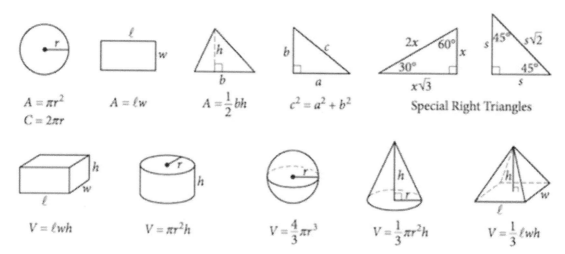

$A = \pi r^2$ $A = \ell w$ $A = \frac{1}{2} bh$ $c^2 = a^2 + b^2$ Special Right Triangles

$C = 2\pi r$

$V = \ell wh$ $V = \pi r^2 h$ $V = \frac{4}{3}\pi r^3$ $V = \frac{1}{3}\pi r^2 h$ $V = \frac{1}{3}\ell wh$

The number of degrees of arc in a circle is 360.
The number of radians of arc in a circle is 2π.
The sum of the measures in degrees of the angles of a triangle is 180.

1. Assume l and m are parallel horizontal lines where l is above m. A third straight line k intersects both lines l and m, creating a total of 4 different angles on each of the two intersections. The intersections of lines l and m contain angles a, b, c, d and w, x, y, z, respectively. The angle layouts start with a and w in the top left position with the other angles following in alphabetical order in the clockwise direction. What is the degree value of angle z if angle c has a value of 67 degrees?

   A. 90 degrees

   B. 180 degrees

C. 67 degrees

D. 113 degrees

2. How to Find the Angle of Two Lines

Angle ∠ABC measures 20°

BD−→− is the bisector of ∠ABC

BE−→ is the bisector of ∠CBD

What is the measure of ∠ABE?

Possible Answers:

A. 5°
B. 15°
C. 40°
D. 30°

3. Aristotle High School has an unusual track in that it is shaped like a regular pentagon with a perimeter one third of a mile. Jessica starts at Point A and runs clockwise until she gets halfway between Points D and E. Which of the following choices is closest to the number of feet she runs?

Possible Answers:

A. 1,300 feet
B. 1,200 feet
C. 1,100 feet
D. 1,000 feet

4. Aristotle High School has an unusual track in that it is shaped like a regular pentagon. Each side of the pentagon measures 264 feet.

Benny runs at a steady speed of eight miles an hour for ten minutes, starting at point A and working his way clockwise. When he is finished, which of the following points is he closest to?

Possible Answers:

A. Point A

B. Point E

C. Point D

D. Point C

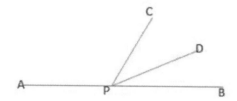

Figure not drawn to scale.

5. In the figure above, APB forms a straight line. If the measure of angle APC is eighty-one degrees larger than the measure of angle DPB, and the measures of angles CPD and DPB are equal, then what is the measure, in degrees, of angle CPB?

Possible Answers:

A. 66

B. 114

C. 50

D. 40

6. One-half of the measure of the supplement of angle ABC is equal to the twice the measure of angle ABC. What is the measure, in degrees, of the complement of angle ABC?

Possible Answers:

    A. 18

    B. 36

    C. 90

    D. 54

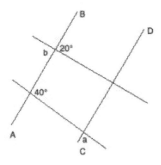

7. In the diagram, AB || CD. What is the value of a+b?

Possible Answers:

    A. 60°

    B. 140°

    C. 80°

    D. 160°

8. In a rectangle ABCD, both diagonals are drawn and intersect at point E.

Let the measure of angle AEB equal x degrees.

Let the measure of angle BEC equal y degrees.

Let the measure of angle CED equal z degrees.

Find the measure of angle AED in terms of x, y, and/or z.

Possible Answers:

   A. $360 - x + y + z$

   B. $180 - 2(x + z)$

   C. $180 - 1/2(x + z)$

   D. $180 - (x + y + z)$

9. A student creates a challenge for his friend. He first draws a square, the adds the line for each of the 2 diagonals. Finally, he asks his friend to draw the circle that has the most intersections possible. How many intersections will this circle have?

Possible Answers:

   A. 4

   B. 6

   C. 8

   D. 12

10. Two pairs of parallel lines intersect:

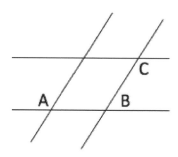

If A = 135°, what is 2 x |B-C| = ?

Possible Answers:

   A. 180°

B. 140°

C. 160°

D. 170°

11. Lines AC and BD are parallel. ∠HFC=10°, ∠DGI=50°, ΔEFG is a right triangle, and EG has a length of 10. What is the length of EF?

Possible Answers:

A. 15

B. 12

C. 5

D. 20

12. If ∠A measures (40−10x)°, which of the following is equivalent to the measure of the supplement of ∠A ?

Possible Answers:

A. (100x)°

B. (50−10x)°

C. (10x+140)°

D. (10x+50)°

13. In the following diagram, lines b and c are parallel to each other. What is the value for x?

Possible Answers:

A. 60∘

B. 30∘

C. It cannot be determined

D. 80∘

14. The measure of the supplement of angle A is 40 degrees larger than twice the measure of the complement of angle A. What is the sum, in degrees, of the measures of the supplement and complement of angle A?

Possible Answers:

    A. 40

    B. 90

    C. 140

    D. 190

15. If $8a - 2 = 22$, then $4a - 1 =$

    A. 2

    B. 14

    C. 11

    D. 12

16. Twenty percent of the sweaters in a store are white. Of the remaining sweaters, 40 percent are brown, and the rest are blue. If there are 200 sweaters in the store, then how many more blue sweaters than white sweaters are in the store?

    A. 56

    B. 54

    C. 23

    D. 64

17. Jill has received 8 of her 12 evaluation scores. So far, Jill's average (arithmetic mean) is 3.75 out of a possible 5. If Jill needs an average of 4.0 points to get a promotion, which list of scores will allow Jill to receive her promotion?

Indicate all such sets.

A. 3.0, 3.5, 4.75, 4.75

B. 3.5, 4.75, 4.75, 5.0

C. 3.25, 4.5, 4.75, 5.0

D. 3.75, 4.5, 4.75, 5.0

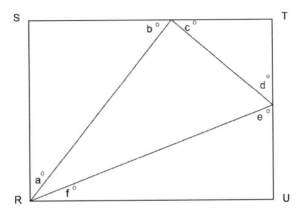

18. In the figure above, if *RSTU* is a rectangle, what is the value of $a + b + c + d + e + f$?

A. 270

B. 180

C. 90

D. 360

19. All first-year students at Red State University must take calculus, English composition, or both. If half of the 2,400 first-year students at Red State University take calculus and half do not, and one-third of those who take calculus also take English composition, how many students take English composition?

A. 400

B. 800

C. 1,200

D. 1,600

20. If the probability of choosing 2 red marbles without replacement from a bag of only red and blue marbles is 3/55 and there are 3 red marbles in the bag, what is the total number of marbles in the bag?

A. 10

B. 11

C. 55

D. 110

21. $5x + 3 = 7x - 1$. Find x

A. 1/3

B. 1/2

C. 1

D. 2

22. $5x + 2(x + 7) = 14x - 7$. Find x

A. 1

B. 2

C. 3

D. 4

23. $12t - 10 = 14t + 2$. Find t

A. -6

B. -4

C. 4

D. 6

24. 5(z + 1) = 3(z + 2) + 11 Solve for z

   A. 2

   B. 4

   C. 6

   D. 12

25. The price of a book went up from $20 to $25. By how many percent did the price increase?

   A. 5

   B. 10

   C. 20

   D. 25

26. The price of a book decreased from $25 to $20. By how many percent did the price decrease?

   A. 5

   B. 10

   C. 20

   D. 25

27. After taking several practice tests, Brian improved the results of his SAT test by 30%. Given that the first time he took the test Brian had answered 150 questions correctly, how many correct answers did he answer in the second test?

   A. 105

   B. 120

   C. 180

   D. 195

28. A number is increased by 2 and then multiplied by 3. The result is 24. What is this number?

    A. 4

    B. 6

    C. 8

    D. 10

29. My father's age divided by 5 is equal to my brother's age divided by 3. My brother is 3 years older than me. My father's age is 3 less than 2 times my age. How old is my father?

    A. 34

    B. 45

    C. 56

    D. 61

30. $(x - 2) / 4 - (3x + 5) / 7 = -3$, $x = ?$

    A. 6

    B. 7

    C. 10

    D. 13

The following questions are numberical answer questions. You need to write down the correct answer. In the exam you will need to fill in your bubble sheet with the numerical answer.

31. $1 / (1 + 1 / (1 - 1/x)) = 4$, $x = ?$

32. Angle A and B are complementary. The measure of angle B is three times the measure of angle A. What is the measure of angle A and B in degrees?

33. What does 68% equal, as a decimal?

34. What is the missing number in the sequence: 4, 6, 10, 18, ___, 66?

35. Simplify the expression: 5,344−57

36. Solve the equation: 3(x−4) =18

37. ABCD is a parallelogram such that AB is parallel to DC and DA parallel to CB. The length of side AB is 10 cm. E is a point between A and B such that the length of AE is 3 cm. F is a point between points D and C. Find the length of DF such that the segment EF divide the parallelogram in two regions with equal areas.

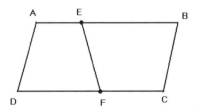

38. Find the measure of angle A in the figure below.

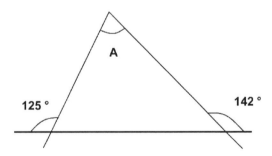

Section 5: SAT Essay Prompt

Directions: You will have 50 mins to prepare an essay in response to the following prompt.

Adapted from Dana Gioia, "Why Literature Matters" ©2005 by The New York Times Company. Originally published April 10, 2005.

A strange thing has happened in the American arts during the past quarter century. While income rose to unforeseen levels, college attendance ballooned, and access to information increased enormously, the interest young Americans showed in the arts—and especially literature—actually diminished.

According to the 2002 Survey of Public Participation in the Arts, a population study designed and commissioned by the National Endowment for the Arts (and executed by the US Bureau of the Census), arts participation by Americans has declined for eight of the nine major forms that are measured....The declines have been most severe among younger adults (ages 18–24). The most worrisome finding in the 2002 study, however, is the declining percentage of Americans, especially young adults, reading literature.

That individuals at a time of crucial intellectual and emotional development bypass the joys and challenges of literature is a troubling trend. If it were true that they substituted histories, biographies, or political works for literature, one might not worry. But book reading of any kind is falling as well.

That such a longstanding and fundamental cultural activity should slip so swiftly, especially among young adults, signifies deep transformations in contemporary life. To call attention to the trend, the Arts Endowment issued the reading portion of the Survey as a separate report, "Reading at Risk: A Survey of Literary Reading in America."

The decline in reading has consequences that go beyond literature. The significance of reading has become a persistent theme in the business world. The February issue of "Wired" magazine, for example, sketches a new set of mental skills and habits proper to the 21st century, aptitudes decidedly literary in character: not "linear, logical, analytical talents," author Daniel Pink states, but "the ability to create artistic and emotional beauty, to detect patterns and opportunities, to craft a satisfying narrative." When asked what kind of talents they like to see in management positions, business leaders consistently set imagination, creativity, and higher-order thinking at the top.

Ironically, the value of reading and the intellectual faculties that it inculcates appear most clearly as active and engaged literacy declines. There is now a growing awareness of the consequences of nonreading to the workplace. In 2001 the National Association of Manufacturers polled its members on skill deficiencies among employees. Among hourly workers, poor reading skills ranked second, and 38 percent of employers complained that local schools inadequately taught reading comprehension.

The decline of reading is also taking its toll in the civic sphere....A 2003 study of 15- to 26-year-olds' civic knowledge by the National Conference of State Legislatures concluded, "Young people do not understand the ideals of citizenship... and their appreciation and support of American democracy is limited."

It is probably no surprise that declining rates of literary reading coincide with declining levels of historical and political awareness among young people. One of the surprising findings of "Reading at Risk" was that literary readers are markedly more civically engaged than nonreaders, scoring two to four times more likely to perform charity work, visit a museum, or attend a sporting event. One reason for their higher social and cultural interactions may lie in the kind of civic and historical knowledge that comes with literary reading....

The evidence of literature's importance to civic, personal, and economic health is too strong to ignore. The decline of literary reading foreshadows serious long-term social and economic problems, and it is time to bring literature and the other arts into discussions of public policy. Libraries, schools, and public agencies do noble work, but addressing the reading issue will require the leadership of politicians and the business community as well....

Reading is not a timeless, universal capability. Advanced literacy is a specific intellectual skill and social habit that depends on a great many educational, cultural, and economic factors. As more Americans lose this capability, our nation becomes less informed, active, and independent-minded. These are not the qualities that a free, innovative, or productive society can afford to lose.

Write an essay in which you explain how Dana Gioia builds an argument to persuade his audience that the decline of reading in America will have a negative effect on society. In your essay, analyze how Gioia uses one or more of the features in the directions that precede the passage (or features of your own choice) to strengthen the logic and persuasiveness of his argument. Be sure that your analysis focuses on the most relevant features of the passage.

Your essay should not explain whether you agree with Gioia's claims, but rather explain how Gioia builds an argument to persuade his audience.

Answers

Section 1: SAT Reading

1. Correct answer: D.

Manning's work exemplifies how biography can be a powerful tool for a historian of science, who can use the genre to explore the effects of politics, economics, and emotions on the direction of scientific development.

This passage is mainly about the effectiveness of biography as a genre for exploring the history of science and the importance of analyzing scientific discoveries from a historical perspective. The business about Black Apollo is just an example the author uses to illustrate his point. So Choice A. is wrong because the passage's main point isn't the importance of Ernest Everett Just. Choice B. is a point the author makes in the last paragraph, but it's not the entire passage's main point. Choice C. appears in the second paragraph, but once again, it doesn't cover the whole passage. Choice D. looks like the right answer; it sums up the overarching theme of the passage.

2. Correct answer: A.

illuminate the effects of social forces on scientists in a way that scientists themselves are unlikely to do

According to the author, "One of the central principles of the history of science, indeed a central reason for the discipline, is to show that science is a product of social forces." That makes Choice A. look like a very good answer. Choice B. isn't exactly right. The author says people can learn scientific theories by reading the work of the scientists themselves. The drawback is that the picture given by scientists is incomplete because it ignores historical context. Choice C. is also imprecise. Historians of science do write biographies, but biographies are just one way to accomplish their main goal of revealing the social forces behind scientific discovery. Choice D. is wrong because the author never suggests that historians of science want to influence scientific research. Choice A. is right.

3.   Correct answer:C.

to explain why biography is both a popular historical genre and a powerful medium for explaining the significance of scientific discoveries

The second paragraph contains a discussion of biography as a historical genre and lists its many advantages. Choice A. isn't at all the main point. It just barely appears in the paragraph. Choice B. is wrong; the author does believe biography is a good historical form for the historian of science. Choice C. looks like a good answer. Choice D. is incorrect; the author says that biographies are very good for teaching children. Choice C. is right.

4.   Correct answer:A.

One of the best ways to come to an understanding of the realities of race relations and scientific development in the 20th century is to read an in-depth account of the life of one of the people who lived and worked in that world.

Choice A. looks pretty good; this is in fact what the author has been saying about the history of science. Choice B. is wrong. The author doesn't think historians should glorify their subjects and notes that Manning doesn't glorify Just. Choice C. is also wrong. The author doesn't imply that a scientific history should downplay science simply because it's "history." Choice D. isn't right. The author explicitly says that Just wasn't the most significant scientist of his time. Choice A. is the best answer.

5.   Correct answer: D.

Just's daily experiences illuminate the conditions characterized by both scientific research and racial relations during his lifetime.

Here's what the passage says: "A comprehensive appreciation of the conditions that Just faced in his daily work offers a powerful lens through which to examine the development of science and racial boundaries in America." Choice D. looks like the answer that matches best with this statement. The other answers are all true, but they're also incidental, facts that add up to a bigger picture but by themselves aren't enough to create a significant history.

6.   Correct answer: D.

the straightforward organization of a biography, which follows the course of the subject's life

A biography is a story of a person's life; the format can't change that much. The author says, "Biographies simply tell a story." The phrase "simplicity of form" doesn't refer to language, so Choice A. is wrong, nor does it mean page design, so Choice B. is wrong. It doesn't mean simple writing style, so Choice C. is wrong. All the author means is that biographies have a standard format, which is fairly consistent from book to book; that makes Choice D. correct.

7. Correct answer: C.

SLS and SLES are detergents that are commonly used in personal care products because they are effective and safe, despite unsubstantiated rumors to the contrary.

This passage introduces the reader to a couple of detergents commonly used in numerous household products. It describes how they work and mentions a few hazards associated with them. The reason the author mentions those hazards in the second paragraph is to get the facts in ahead of the risks that are solely based on rumor, because her point in the last paragraph is that many of the things people fear about SLS and SLES aren't based on fact. She obviously thinks SLS and SLES are safe as they're commonly used and believes that approval by the FDA and other scientific organizations is sufficient proof of this safety.

Choice A. is a possible answer, but it ignores the discussion of Internet detractors, so it doesn't cover the entire passage. Look for something with a more global application. Choice B. is wrong. The presence of "despite" suggests that the author thinks incorporating SLS or SLES into personal care products is irresponsible or dangerous, which isn't justified by the passage. Choice C. looks like a better answer than Choice A. because it incorporates more of the passage's information. Choice D. is wrong because this passage isn't about the Internet rumors but about counteracting them. Choice C. is the best answer.

8. Correct answer: B.

shampoo, toothpaste, bathroom cleaners, and engine degreasers

You have to read carefully to answer this one. Don't assume any product contains the substances unless the passage tells you so. If you prefer, you can underline or circle substances that the author mentions in the passage in the answer choices — that makes it easier to see the ones that appear in the text. Choice A. is wrong because the author never mentions mouthwash, sunscreen, or hair dye. Choice B. looks good. They're all mentioned in the passage. Choice C. is wrong because the passage doesn't mention engine lubricants. Choice D. is wrong because moisturizer and baby wipes don't appear. Choice B. is correct.

9.   Correct answer: D.

refute claims that SLS and SLES are dangerous

The author says that the rumors about SLS and SLES are absurd and unsubstantiated and "the FDA has approved the use of SLS and SLES in a number of personal care products." That means she's using FDA approval as evidence of the substances' safety. Choice A. looks like a possible answer, though it doesn't mention the author's suggestion that the FDA approval implies safety, so it misses the reason why the author brings up the FDA. Choice B. is wrong because even though the author thinks that the FDA has the best interests of consumers in mind, that isn't the reason why the author mentions the FDA. The purpose of mentioning the FDA is to provide evidence debunking the Internet myths. Choice C. doesn't work because the author isn't in fact suggesting that FDA approval of putting SLS and SLES in personal care products means that manufacturers don't have to test these products for safety. Choice D. works the best because the author mentions the FDA to achieve the larger goal of debunking the Internet rumors.

10. Correct answer: D.

burning eyes, burned skin after long exposure, and diarrhea if ingested in large quantities

Read the passage carefully. The answers to this question appear in the second paragraph, not in the third paragraph, which lists risks that haven't been proven. Skim the answer choices to cross off anything that appears in the third paragraph. Choice D. is the right answer. Every other choice contains ailments that Internet rumors have associated with SLS and SLES but that haven't been substantiated.

11. Correct answer: D.

a description of SLS and SLES and their uses; known risks of SLS and SLES; criticisms aimed at SLS and SLES by detractors on the Internet; evidence that SLS and SLES are safe and the rumors unfounded

Look for an answer that could function as an accurate ordering of all paragraphs in the passage. Choice A. isn't quite right because it leaves off the subject of the first paragraph. Choice B. is wrong. The passage doesn't contain any anecdotal accounts of SLS injuries. Choice C. doesn't work because the first paragraph doesn't describe the chemical composition of SLS and SLES. Choice D. is the best answer because it follows the structure of the passage closely.

12. Correct answer: D.

to explain why some people fear SLS and SLES and to list the diseases that Internet rumors have linked to the substances

The third paragraph discusses the Internet rumors that hold SLS and SLES responsible for a host of ailments without providing proof. The author obviously wants to discredit these rumors; that's what the last sentence is all about. She's not criticizing, so Choice A. is out. She's not describing the substances — that's in the first paragraph — so Choice B. is out. She doesn't believe these risks are real, so she's not warning anyone of anything, and Choice C. is out. She makes no proposals of alternate substances, so Choice D is the best answer here.

13. Correct answer: A.

It is unreasonable for people to be afraid of substances that have been deemed safe by the FDA and several other major organizations, and that have a long history of safe use, simply on the basis of unsubstantiated rumors.

Choice A. looks like a good possibility. The author does seem to think it's silly to believe rumors about substances that people have been using safely for years. Choice B. doesn't quite work. The author does trust the FDA but makes no mention of its sources of funding or mission. Choice C. is wrong. While the author clearly thinks that some Internet information isn't trustworthy, the passage doesn't provide sufficient information for you to infer how she feels about information available about other health topics. For example, she could easily think that the Internet supplies good information on heart disease. Choice D. doesn't work. The author does think SLS and SLES are cheap and effective surfactants and emulsifiers, but she doesn't think that they're unsafe to use in products that contact human skin. Choice A. is the best answer.

14. Correct answer: D.

the amount of time that has passed since the eyewitness experienced the event

Answer this question by eliminating answers that Passage A indicates have been researched to discover their effect on the accuracy of eyewitness testimony. The third paragraph comes right out and tells you that race, gender, and age have been studied, so Choices A and B are ruled out. The second paragraph states that "much research" has been done on the effects of witnesses who are asked misleading questions. A misleading question is a type of question, so you can infer that the effect of the question type on eyewitness accounts has been studied and cross out Choice C. You can reasonably assume that the amount of time that passes between an event and an eyewitness's account of that event would affect the accuracy of the testimony, but the question doesn't ask for your reasonable assumption. Because Passage A doesn't mention any studies conducted to see how time affects eyewitness testimony, Choice D. offers the exception. Remember to answer questions based solely on information in the passage, regardless of any outside or personal knowledge you may have on the subject matter.

15. Correct answer: B.

Eyewitness testimony is often flawed because it is influenced by a variety of factors.

The best answer incorporates a point suggested by both passages. Eliminate answers that can be supported by only one of the passages. Passage A makes the statement that there's no difference between the accuracy of male and female testimony, but Passage B doesn't discuss the role of gender, so Choice D. is supported by only one passage and can't be right. Although both passages mention that eyewitness testimony is affected by a number of variables, only Passage B discusses the importance of determining an error rate. Neither passage discusses how memory improves or declines over time, so Choice C. is out of contention. That leaves Choices A. and B. Choice A. doesn't seem likely. The first line of Passage A states that "there are many factors that may account for mistaken eyewitness identification" and then goes on to describe the research of these factors, which implies that mistaken eyewitness identification occurs frequently enough to warrant significant study. Passage B stresses the science of memory and human cognitive abilities and states that they're "not perfect." In the third paragraph, the author of Passage B points out that establishing an error rate involves an awareness of the many factors that affect eyewitness accounts. Neither passage suggests that eyewitness testimony is "highly" accurate, but both imply that accounts may be flawed by the influence of several factors or variables. Because it's a better answer than Choice A., Choice B. is correct.

16. Correct answer: A.

How the lighting in a particular event affects the reliability of eyewitness identification is a variable that warrants a good amount of study.

Your job is to eliminate reasonable implications of Passage A. The passage tells you that one's race can affect how well one recognizes someone's face, so it implies that one's race may adversely affect the reliability of an identification. Cross out Choice B. The passage justifies the statement in Choice C. It categorizes the factors as system variables and estimator variables. So Choice C. is wrong. The passage states that the majority of research has gone into studying system variables, and the makeup of a lineup is a system variable. So you can reasonably infer Choice D. from the statements in Passage A. The passage tells you that the way questions are worded is a system variable, and the judicial system has control over system variables. Therefore, the author of Passage A must think that the judicial system has control over whether a witness is asked misleading questions. Choice A. must be the answer. Passage A states that lighting can affect an eyewitness identification, but because lighting is an estimator variable over which the judicial system has little control, it's unlikely to receive much research. The passage states that system variables receive the majority of study. The best answer is Choice A.

17. Correct answer: D

To understand how memory and human cognitive abilities are affected by a variety of different factors

Both passages discuss memory and how it's affected by different factors; what differs is the factors they discuss. Passage A covers variables that include the age, race, and gender of eyewitnesses and the wording of the questions they're asked. Passage B emphasizes the complexity of memory and cognitive abilities. Rule out choices that pertain to one passage but not the other. Choice A. is a concern of Passage B but isn't mentioned in Passage A, so it's wrong. Choice C is important to Passage A but not to Passage B. Choice B. isn't a goal of either passage. Passage B does indeed mention episodic memory, aside from defining the term, the passage doesn't show how the concept contributes to judicial proceedings. By process of elimination, the best answer is Choice D. Both passages deal with the complex factors that affect cognitive ability and memory as they relate to the accuracy of eyewitness testimony.

18. Correct answer: D.

Both passages concern improving eyewitness accuracy, but Passage A focuses on controlling variables and Passage B concentrates on understanding the science behind human recollection.

You can eliminate some answers quickly because they aren't true. Choice A. is wrong because Passage B doesn't discuss witness questioning and therefore doesn't dismiss its importance. Choice B. isn't right because how the judicial system controls certain variables is a concern of Passage A, not Passage B. because both passages deal with how research can improve eyewitness accuracy: through research of system variables for Passage A and the establishment of an error rate in Passage B. Choice C. may be tempting because Passage A mentions the effect of race on eyewitness identification, but the way the question is worded implies that Passage B does indeed discuss race, at least to some degree, which is inaccurate. Choice D. is the only option that appropriately defines a noticeable difference between the content of the two passages. The primary focus of Passage A is the variables that affect the accuracy of eyewitness identification. Passage B is more concerned with the workings of the human mind and how this knowledge can be used to establish an error rate for witness testimony. Choice D. is best.

19. Correct answer: D.

Lighting issues and the length of time someone witnessed an event are examples of system variables.

This question asks you for the statement that isn't supported by either passage. Eliminate answers that appear in either of the two passages. Choice A.is a premise of both passages; they both state that human memory doesn't get it right every time. Passage B says that eyewitness memory should make "guilty people seem more likely to be guilty," and Choice C. seems to paraphrase that statement. Passage B's first paragraph states that cognitive abilities are incredible and supports that statement with the assertion that visual, auditory, olfactory, tactile, and taste information synchronizes with past information to bring that information into the present, so the statement in Choice B. is supported by Passage B. If you thought Choice D. was supported by Passage A, you confused system variables with estimator variables. Lighting issues and the length of time someone witnessed an event are actually examples of estimator variables. Choice D. is the answer that neither passage supports.

20. Correct answer: C.

the philosophical origins of public schools in 18th century Germany and the transformation in educational thinking in the 19th century.

This passage is about the origins of public education and the changes that occurred in educational philosophy in the first century of public schools; the whole thing is set in Germany. Choice A. doesn't cover the whole passage; the political message seems to apply only to the first half. Choice B. also focuses on just the first half and so isn't the passage's primary point. The final paragraph doesn't focus on exploitation at all. Choice C. conveys the passage's overarching theme. Choice D. is wrong because the passage doesn't get into modern educational practices. Choice C. is correct.

21. Correct answer: C.

They were indifferent to the well-being and needs of their workers, caring only to maximize production and profits no matter what it cost their employees.

The author tells you that textile mill owners exploited their workers badly enough to incite revolts and that they embraced the concept of schools in the hopes that it would make the workers more docile. Choice A. is quite wrong. The first schools weren't created to help the students so much as to help the nobles. Choice B. could well be true, but the passage doesn't discuss it. Remember, all correct answers must not stray too far from the text. Choice C. fits well with what the passage says about the owners. It does appear that they were indifferent to the well-being of their workers. Choice D. isn't quite right. The passage doesn't specifically tell you that they were all aristocrats. Although some of them may have believed their authority was divinely ordained, you can't assume that was true of them all, nor is there any reason for you to assume that they cared about nurturing their workers. Choice C. is the best answer.

22. Correct answer: B.

Eighteenth-century schools were concerned primarily with teaching working-class children to accept their fate and love their ruler; 19th-century schools began to focus on developing the full human potential of students.

The educational difference between the two centuries was philosophical. Schools in the 1700s were meant for workers and intended to instill patriotism and gratitude toward the government into their students, but schools in the 1800s aspired to develop children to their full potential. Choice A. isn't right because 18th-century schools had nothing to do with efficient textile mills. Choice B. looks like a very good answer. Choice C. doesn't work because 18th-century schools were for the children of workers, not the aristocracy, and in the 19th century, no one had to spin anymore. Choice D. is tricky because it's very close to being correct, but the passage doesn't tell you that 19th-century schools aspired to create free-thinking students in general (though academic freedom was prized for advanced students), so it's wrong. Choice B. is the right answer.

23. Correct answer: A.

riots and other forms of violence against the owners of textile factories by peasants unhappy at their treatment.

Look at the sentence after the one that mentions increasing levels of unrest. It says that the rulers wanted "to channel the energy of restless peasants into something that would be less dangerous to the throne than riots." So "unrest" must mean riots and other violent uprisings by workers who disliked their lot in life. That would be Choice A. None of the other answers work. Choice A. is correct.

24. Correct answer: D.

They liked the idea because it would make the peasantry more complacent and accepting of their fate, which would help keep the aristocracy safe in their prosperity.

According to the passage: "Aristocrats liked this idea. They liked the thought of schools making peasants more docile and patriotic, and they appreciated the way state-run schools would teach children of lower social classes to accept their position in life." Choice A. is wrong because the schools were intended to do just the opposite; educating workers was supposed to make them more docile, not more violent. Choice B. doesn't work because the passage never mentions aristocratic resentment of taxes. Choice C. may be a true statement, but the passage doesn't directly come out and say it. You know nothing of the aristocratic opinions of Schlabrendorff himself. Choice D. is the most suitable answer to this question.

25. Correct answer: B.

to take away the authority of parents and replace it with state power over children and citizens.

The truant officers were meant to take away parental authority over children and replace it with state control. Choice B. is the most accurate answer. The truant officers weren't there to make sure every child was educated, so Choice A. is wrong. They didn't help or indoctrinate parents or children, nor did they recruit boys into the army, which nixes Choices C. and D. Choice B. is best.

26. Correct answer: D.

People learn best in an environment that respects their individuality, affords them freedom, and incorporates a variety of aspects of learning, such as physical movement, manual skills, and independent exploration.

Nineteenth-century educational theorists believed in nurturing innate abilities and using holistic techniques. That's not Choice A. In fact, Choice A. is just the opposite of what experts thought in the 1800s. Choice B. is wrong because nothing in the passage mentions religion. Choice C. isn't right. The passage never suggests that the state has an interest in an educated citizenry, just an interest in a docile and patriotic one, and that wasn't the prevailing view in the 19th century anyway. Choice D. looks like a perfect answer to this question. That makes Choice D. correct.

27. Correct answer: A.

The purpose of the passage is to discuss ECP

    A. and why it was enacted.

    B. This is an issue that is addressed in the passage, but it is not the major issue of the passage.

    C. The brilliance of the drafters cannot be said to have been exalted. Instead, the ECPA is said to be confusing and unusually complicated.

    D. This statement is not made by the passage.

28. Correct answer: D.

Public network service providers are said to be indifferent to the rights of their users because the providers are so tenuously connected to the users.

    A. This word is not an accurate description.

    B. The service providers do not completely ignore the rights of their users; they are just disinclined to jump through legal hoops to protect those rights.

    C. This word is not an accurate description.

    D. Correct

29. Correct answer: D.

The author describes how the added importance and growth of cyberspace has created legal issues regarding privacy that are not covered by the Fourth Amendment. In order to protect the spirit of the Constitution, ECPA was drafted to outline the rights of Internet users.

    A. This statement was not made in the passage. It was merely said that they are easier to gain than search warrants.

    B. The passage does not say that service providers protect no rights, just that they do not protect the rights of privacy zealously.

    C. This statement is not really supported by the passage; the ECPA protects rights where they deserve to be protected, not where there is a "need for privacy."

30. Correct answer: B.

It was hard to tell what the Fourth Amendment would and would not allow in cyberspace.

    A. The opposite was stated.

    (C–D). These words do not describe the effects of the Fourth Amendment.

31. Correct answer: D.

The purpose was to contrast that which the Fourth Amendment was designed to protect with that which it is currently being used to protect, namely, computers on the Internet.

    A. This statement is partially true, but this is not a place where the gaps would be filled in.

    B. There is no mention of cyber homes in the passage.

    C. This is not the case.

32. Correct answer: B.

This is stated explicitly

    A. This point is not stated or implied by the pas-sage.

    C. The opposite is stated to be true.

    D. This statement is not true. The Fourth Amendment still applies to our homes.

33. Correct answer: D.

The passage relates the facts surrounding the dissolution of the U.S.S.R, and Russia's reemergence onto the global scene. It goes on to tell how Russia has had to change in order to adapt to the new system of government.

    A. This description was true of the other governments also.

    B. It was never stated that this was the only thing wrong with Russian politics.

    C. It was not stated that the inability to tap into Siberian resources hurt the Soviet Union in any way.

34. Correct answer: D.

    A. The Russian Federation came into existence after 1991.

B. According to the passage, Yeltsin came onto the scene after 1991.

C. Europe did not break up the Soviet Union. The Soviet Union was destroyed in an internal coup.

35. Correct answer: C.

The "monolithic union" refers to the unified states under the Soviet Union.

A. The word monolithic is used to describe "unwieldy" and "large" instead of "stone."

B. This could be correct if the date preceded 1991, but afterward there was no sense of indestructibility.

D. This point is not mentioned in the passage.

36. Correct answer: A.

This passage explains the implications of the breakup of the Soviet Union.

B. The passage makes no such claim.

C. There is no explanation of the short-term goals of the smaller republics.

D. This point was hinted at by the paragraph, but the purpose of the paragraph is to explain how the states would need to reorganize, not to cast blame.

37. Correct answer: A.

This view was shown by their preference to avoid living in Siberia.

B. This statement is not true. There is thought to be almost a vacuum of power in the region since the fall of the Soviet Union.

C. This inference is not accurate.

D. This is a contradiction in terms. Favorably desolate?

38. Correct answer: D.

Nothing is said about Russia currently being benevolent or corruption free.

A. The passage makes this point

B. The passage makes this point.

C. The passage makes this point

39. Correct answer: C

One general class, one division, and one section.

This question is asking for a detail stated in the passage. The Dewey Decimal System is outlined in the first paragraph, which states that titles are arranged "into 10 classes, with 10 divisions each, with each division having 10 sections." This matches answer choice (C). Choices (A) and (B) each omit at least one part, and choice (D) would be found in the Library of Congress Classification.

40. Correct answer: B

Named after a person

The question is asking for the meaning of a word as used in the passage. Research the first sentence for context clues. This sentence introduces Melvil Dewey and the system that carries his name. Answer choice (B) clearly relates to the meaning of the sentence. There is no suggestion that the new system was the most important one or uniquely innovative (it could have been based on a previous system), making (A) and (C) incorrect. Nothing in the passage indicates that the Dewey Decimal System is logical and simple to use, as in (D).

41. Correct Answer: D

by Date of Acquisition

This is stated in the passage.

42. Correct answer: A

500

This is stated in the passage

43. Correct answer: D

Rustic Campsite in February

The question asks for an inference about the least expensive accommodations. Research the passage for information about rates. The next-to-last sentence notes that all accommodations are less expensive during the off season, so you can infer that choice (A) is less expensive than (B) and that choice (D). is less expensive than (C). Eliminate (B) and (C). Now determine which costs less, the Simple Bungalow or the Rustic Campsite. The passage introduces the cabins by saying they are appropriate for those with "the budget for a few amenities." (Amenities are comforts or conveniences.) This statement suggests that the indoor options are more expensive than the preceding outdoor options. Thus, you can infer that a Rustic Campsite rents for a lower rate than a Simple Bungalow, and choice (D) is correct.

44. Correct answer: C

None although there is a closed season, the passage indicates the park is open all year.

45. Correct answer: C.

Telephone

This is stated in the passage.

46. Correct answer: A.

Families

This is implied in the passage.

47. Correct answer: A.

Luxury Cottage

This is implied in the passage, although not explicitly stated.

48. Correct answer: C

The passage was written to analyze the works by Chang-Rae Lee and the themes presented in his most famous novels.

49. Correct answer: A

The author of this passage uses the first line of the novel to provide an example of one of the themes of the novel.

50. Correct answer: B

Espionage is part of the plot of the novel Native Speaker, but it is not a theme that recurs in Lee's works.

51. Correct answer: D

The passage states that Lee's interests in cultural identity and race emerge from his own experiences with these issues as a young immigrant to America.

52. Correct answer: D

The tone of the last paragraph suggests concern over the preservation of cultural identities in an increasingly mixed and expanding world.

Section 2: SAT Writing and Language

1. Correct answer: B

Since the "Fair" is mentioned before the comma, there is no need to repeat the word after the comma. B. correctly uses the past tense verb, "originated," and the modifier "which".

2. Correct answer: A

"When" can only refer to time. Since a specific year is mentioned just prior to the usage of this word, we can determine that it is being used correctly in this sentence. "After which" does not make sense with the word "originated" that appears in this sentence. "As" means "because" in this context, and also does not make sense in the sentence.

3. Correct answer: D

Since the paragraph mentions the festival takes place "each year," we need a verb to reflect that meaning. "Took" is past tense. "Had taken" is past perfect tense, and "did take place" implies an event that occurred in the past but does not continue into the present.

4. Correct answer: C

Since "stunning" and "beautiful" are so similar in meaning, this pairing can be considered redundant. Avoid redundancy on the SAT English Writing and Language Test! A simple "beautiful" is sufficient to express the intended meaning. The words "yet" and "however" both imply a contrast, but these words are similar, not contrasting.

5. Correct answer: D

The verb tenses here must agree and both be in past tense. D. Correctly uses the past tense "began" and "completed". The past perfect "had" would only be used to refer to an event even further back in the past than a simple past tense event. "Was began" is not correct. In C., the usage of two past perfect verbs creates confusion: which event occurred first? The correct construction should use two simple past tense verbs or one past tense verb and one past perfect verb.

6. **Correct answer: B**

A colon is used to introduce a definition or explanation. A semicolon is used to separate two independent clauses. Since the clause after the comma is dependent (not a complete sentence), the semicolon is incorrect here.

7. **Correct answer: A**

The past tense verb "exited" is parallel with the other past tense verb "was reserved" that appears later in the sentence. The other verbs are not parallel and are in future or present tense.

8. **Correct answer: C**

The correct idiom is "not only...but also." It is not correct to have "not only...but" in an SAT English Writing and Language sentence, nor is it correct to have "not...but also." C. creates a sentence with the correct idiom.

9. **Correct answer: C**

This paragraph focuses on the construction of the Plaza de Toros and the Spanish Royal Family. Note how three of the sentences provide additional information on the Plaza de Toros, while one sentence introduces unnecessary information about the Seville Festival.

10. **Correct answer: D**

The word "and" implies two similar ideas, but the ideas in these two clauses contrast. The phrase "even though" is the best transition phrase for this sentence. The other options create illogical meanings. Only D. creates a clear contrasting meaning.

11. **Correct answer: A**

The past perfect "had been completed" correctly refers to an event that occurred even before another past tense event, so it is correctly used in this sentence. The other tenses are incorrect.

12. **Correct answer: B**

Two independent clauses cannot be separated by a comma. This is called a run-on sentence, or a comma splice. B. corrects the issue by replacing the comma with a semicolon. Simply moving the position of the comma is not enough to correct the run-on, nor is replacing the comma with a dash.

13. Correct answer: C

On the SAT English Writing and Language Test, many sentences will begin with a modifying phrase and a comma. The subject after the comma must be the person or thing doing the action of the modifying phrase. Here it is the architect, Anival Gonzalez, who is "choosing to redo them in brick," so she must come immediately after the comma. D. incorrectly implies the architect took the years 1914-1915 to decide to replace the grandstands, rather than carry out the actual work.

14. Correct answer: C

The pronoun "they" has no clear antecedent in the sentence. For example, is it the armchairs or the builders who were placed in front of theater boxes? Choice D. cannot be correct because the sentence would then read: "and it were placed in front of the theater boxes."

15. Correct answer: A

This sentence nicely brings the passage back to its original theme: the popular, tourist-filled festival. The other choices provide additional historical or tourist information that do not provide a satisfactory conclusion.

16. Correct answer: B

Assuming that they are right next to each other, as they are here, no punctuation is necessary between the subject of a sentence and the main verb. *The different kinds of prairie wildflowers* is our noun phrase (technically, the subject is *kinds*, and *of prairie wildflowers* is a prepositional phrase, but this doesn't make a difference here), and the main verb is *are*.

17. Correct answer: D

This section of the passage is in the present tense, and the subject phrase is *grasses and herbaceous wildflowers*, so the correct form for the main verb is *dominate* (present-tense plural).

18. Correct answer: D

Coneflowers, and how many types there are, are not mentioned anywhere else in this paragraph or the entire passage. The passage is about prairies, not specific types of flowers. Therefore, this sentence would distract from the main idea.

19. Correct answer: A

The entire passage so far has been about the diverse flora found on prairies. The reader would expect that the assertion that prairies are interesting and colorful would have something to do with biodiversity.

20. Correct answer: A

This choice correctly results in an independent clause followed by a dependent clause, with the two clauses separated by a comma.

21. Correct answer: B

Old railroads are the rarest of the four environments offered as choices, and so this choice best establishes that black soil prairies are difficult to find today.

22. Correct answer: C

The implication of the sentence in the context of the paragraph is that it is regrettable that the original prairies have been destroyed. Therefore, *Unfortunately* is the appropriate introductory word.

23. Correct answer: D

The main idea of the paragraph concerns the depletion of gravel prairies, and so a guess that some of these prairies are probably new seems out of place.

24. Correct answer: A

Since the noun *they* performs both the verb *are* and the verb *contain*, no comma is necessary after *degraded*. Furthermore, the information presented in this choice is the most relevant to the paragraph. (In this question, the right and wrong answers are determined by a combination of grammatical and stylistic factors—the test does not do this often, but it does happen, so watch out for it!)

25. Correct answer: C

The antecedent of the pronoun *they* is the noun phrase *gravel and dolomite prairies*. Therefore, sentence 4 should come right after a sentence that makes this apparent. It should also not come between sentences 3 and 5, as sentence 5 is clearly supposed to immediately follow sentence 3. And it makes sense that sentence 4 should be next to sentence 2, as both concern the physical characteristics of gravel and dolomite prairies. Of the choices, only H (which places sentence 4 between sentences 2 and 3) resolves all of these issues.

26. Correct answer: B

This choice correctly separates two independent clauses into two separate sentences by use of a period.

27. Correct answer: D

This choice correctly uses *that* (with no comma) to attach a grammatically correct essential/limiting clause to the pronoun *those*.

28. Correct answer: B

The subject noun *species* is plural here (although the singular form is identical), and so the plural verb *are* is necessary.

29. Correct answer: D

The adjectives *moist*, *mesic*, and *dry* constitute a list of three different things that sand prairies can be. Therefore, commas are necessary after *moist* and *mesic*. (Although the comma before the conjunction that separates the final two items in a list is optional when the conjunction is *and*, it is mandatory when the conjunction is *or*!) The word *dry* ends one independent clause, which then needs to be joined to the subsequent one via a comma + conjunction, and so a comma is also necessary after *dry*.

30. Correct answer: C

The question asks for a "colorful image," and choice C offers us the most vivid and specific image: *purple spiderwort, orange butterfly weed, and yellow goldenrod*.

31. Correct answer: C

The clause is "a bunch of guys from my class started playing paintball," and the additional information "myself included" is inserted into that clause. It needs to be set off with two of the same punctuation marks, and choice C, with two commas, is the only choice that does so.

32. Correct answer: B

We need the word you're (the contraction for "you are") and the word it's (the contraction for "it is"), and choice B is the one that has both. Your and it's are both possessive pronouns, and would be wrong here. (It can be hard to remember this, because apostrophes usually indicate possession, but not with pronouns.) Whenever you're not sure in a situation like this, just substitute you are or it is for the word and see whether it makes sense.

33. Correct answer: B

This answer uses they're ("they are"), which is plural, to replace the antecedent a player, which is singular. Even though we often use they as a gender-neutral singular pronoun when speaking, remember that it is technically grammatically wrong, and therefore wrong on the test! The other trick here is that choice B is the shortest alternative, and we are used to longer choices being wrong due to awkwardness or inefficiency. But whether a choice is grammatically right or wrong is always more important!

34. Correct answer: D

The sentence is in the past tense, and so we need the past-tense form cost. This is a tricky one because, although the story takes place in the past, some of the phrases near this sentence state ongoing truths, and so are in the present tense, like "it's quite an investment" or "Pads aren't necessary." The clues are that this sentence contains the phrase at the time before the underlined part and the word wasn't after it, both of which clearly indicate past tense. Correct answers to verb-tense questions on the SAT usually involve simpler tenses, as opposed to more complex ones.

35. Correct answer: D

This answer contains a single, comprehensible independent clause, preceded by the introductory dependent clause "after your first day." All of the other choices involve chopping up and rearranging this sentence into nonsensical variations on it. With questions like this one, which involve rearranging an entire long sentence, look for the "smoothest" answer, or the one that sounds the most like everyday speech (it is frequently the last choice, but not always).

36. Correct answer: D

Since the sentence "A bunch of protective gear is required too" introduces the topic of protective gear, it should come before the parts that talk about such equipment. But the sentence ends with the word too, which indicates that it comes after some other requirement was stated.

37. Correct answer: A

Although all the choices concern finding a place to play, the beginning of the following sentence implies that a specific location ("It was the only...") has already been chosen. Only choice A settles on a specific location.

38. Correct answer: D

This is the only grammatically correct choice, as it creates two independent clauses and separates them appropriately with a semicolon. It may sound wordy, but the other three choices are grammatically wrong.

39. Correct answer: C

Since the underlined part is preceded by stand between, you know you need two things. The test tries to trick you with the and that occurs later in the sentence, but that is just part of the prepositional phrase (of and everything after it) that adds more information about the nature of the thrill. Choice C has two things and uses the correct us with no comma.

40. Correct answer: A

The sentence is in the present tense (it talks about the memories of the past, not the past itself), and the noun performing the verb here is memories, which is plural, and so you need bring. This is the prepositional phrase trick: the words of my heroism that summer are extra information that can be taken out, so you have to jump over them. Someone who doesn't notice this could be fooled by the word heroism or the word summer, which are both singular.

41. Correct answer: A

We need the plural possessive here. Their having might sound weird, but since having is a gerund, it takes a possessive pronoun. In speech, you would probably be more likely to say "without them having any idea," but this is a test.

42. Correct answer: C

When a sentence should be deleted, it is usually obvious. The underlined sentence is funny, consistent with the author's voice and the mood of the essay, and relevant to the action at this point. There is no reason to get rid of it.

43. Correct answer: B

The author here is speaking in the present tense about the past. He currently does not remember why they stopped playing.

44. Correct Answer B.

The author is reminscing and the word just refers to the relection of the point in his life that the child in question would be experiencing.

Section 3: SAT Math No Calculator

1. Correct answer: D

Because 4^{12} is a common factor of both 4^{13} and 4^{12}, you can rewrite the numerator as 4^{12} (4 − 1). Now look at the whole fraction: You can divide 4^{12} by 4^{11}, leaving you with $4^1(4 − 1)$. Now the calculation should be much easier. $4 \times 3 = 12$, choice (D).

2. Correct answer: D

To solve this expression you need to break apart the factorial of 13 to the common prime number in the denominator, in this case the number 2. 13! can be expressed as $13 \times 12 \times 11 \times 10 \times 9 \times 8 \times 7 \times 6 \times 5 \times 4 \times 3 \times 2 \times 1$. When you break apart this factorial into its prime numbers you are left with $13 \times 11 \times 7 \times 5^2 \times 3^5 \times 2^{10}$. For a fraction to result in an integer, the denominator of the fraction must share at least one prime factor with the numerator, so at minimum there needs to be one 2, so $1 \leq x$. Eliminate (A), (B), and (C). The number of two's that the denominator can have cannot exceed 10 because that is the greatest number of two's in the numerator, so $x \leq 10$. The correct answer is (D).

3. Correct answer: C

The expression in the question is in the form of $x^2 − y^2$, where $4a^2$ corresponds to x^2 and $4b^2$ corresponds to y2. Since $x^2 − y^2$ factors to $(x + y) (x − y)$, $4a^2 − 4b^2$ factors to $(2a)^2 − (2b)^2 = (2a + 2b) (2a − 2b)$.

4. Correct answer: C

$16 + 4x = 24$

$4x = 8$

$x = 2$

But the questions wants 8x

so 8x2 = 16

5. Correct answer: D

$2,600 was the salesman's commission on the fourth sale. Since the average of the four commissions is $2,000, the total must be $2,000 × 4 = $8,000. Subtracting the total of the other three commissions from $8,000 gives the commission on the fourth sale.

6. Correct answer: A

First, isolate each variable. $2a < 6 \rightarrow a < 3$. $3b > 27 \rightarrow b > 9$. Now, assume that $a = 3$ and $b = 9$. In this case, $b - a = 9 - 3 = 6$. Since $a < 3$ and $b > 9$, the difference between the two must *be greater* than 6. Thus, 6 is not a possible value for $b - a$.

7. Correct answer: D

Since triangle ABC is inscribed in a semicircle, it must be a right triangle. The area of the triangle is thus $(1/2) × 10 × 24 = 120$. Using the Pythagorean Theorem, the diameter of the circle = AC = 26. The area of the circle is thus $(\pi)r^2 = (\pi)13^2 = (\pi)169$. The area of the semicircle is thus $(169\pi)/2 = 84.5\pi$. The area of the shaded region = area of the semicircle – area of the triangle. This can be expressed as $84.5\pi - 120$.

8. Correct answer: C

Plug the given values into the R × T = D formula. The rate is 2.6 million feet per day and the distance is 10.2 million feet. Thus: 2.6 million × T = 10.2 million $\rightarrow$ T = (10.2 million/2.6million) = approximately 4 days. Now, convert days to 2.6 million seconds. 1 day = 24 hours = 60(24) minutes = 60(60)(24) seconds = 86,400 seconds. So, the number of seconds in 4 days is 86,400 × 4 = 345,600 seconds. The closest answer is 350,000.

9. Correct answers: C and D

If $x + y = 0$, and neither x nor $y = 0$, then it must be the case that x and y are different numbers with the same absolute value. For example, $x = -2$ and $y = 2$. Based on this example, choices A and B are possible. For choice C to be possible, x and y would have to have the same sign. But they cannot have the same sign since they must cancel each other out. Choice C cannot be true and is thus a possible answer. Choice D cannot be true because any non-zero number raised to an even exponent will yield a positive result. Positive + positive > 0.

10. Correct answers: B, C, and D

If the percentage, when rounded to the nearest tenth, is 14.2%, then the actual percentage, p, is such that $14.15 \le p \le 14.249$. We can use this percentage range to yield a range for the number of voters who expressed a preference for an independent candidate. The lower bound will be 14.15% of 80,000 = 11,320. The upper bound will be 14.249% of 80,000 = 11,399.2. Any value that falls between these two endpoints will be an answer. Among the choices, the values that fall in this range are B, C, and D.

11. Correct answer: D

Refer to the right side and the left side of the "Subscription to Newsmagazine x, 1970-1985" chart. In 1980, Newsmagazine x accounted for 14.6 percent of newsmagazine subscriptions, and it had 7,000 subscriptions.

12. Correct answer: B

In 1981, Newsmagazine z accounted for 9,400 out of 57,000 newsmagazine subscriptions. Therefore, Newsmagazine z accounted for approximately 9,000 out of 57,000, 15.7% of the nationwide newsmagazine subscriptions.

13. Correct answer: D

In 1970, there were 1,500 subscriptions to Newsmagazine x, which accounted for approximately 25 percent of total nationwide subscriptions. Total nationwide subscriptions in 1970, then, were equal to about 6,000 (25 percent of total nationwide subscriptions = 1,500). Using the same process, total nationwide subscriptions in 1971 were equal to about 9,000 (30 percent of total nationwide subscriptions = 2,600). The percent increase between 1970 and 1971 is or 50 percent.

14. Correct answer: C

In 1973, Newsmagazine x had 3,300 subscriptions, or 20.5 percent of the total number of newsmagazine subscriptions. Set up the calculation to find the total: 3,300/20.5 = 160.98. then 160.98 x 100 = 16097. Round to find that x = 16,000.

15. Correct answer: B

The number of students majoring in Philosophy in 2015 was 1.11(1,000) = 1,110. The number of students majoring in Philosophy in 2017 was thus (0.97)(1,110) = 1,076.7 or approximately 1,077.

16. Correct answers: A and B

The easiest way to confirm each choice is to plug in numbers.

Choice A: Choose 1,000 for the number of Psychology majors in 2015. The number of Psychology majors in 2017 was thus 1,000(0.9)(1.1) = 990. Choice A is correct.

Choice B: Choose 1,000 for the number of Mathematics majors in 2015. The number of Mathematics majors in 2017 was thus 1,000(1.06)(1.11) = 1,176. The change was 176. 176 is more than 17% of 1,000, Thus, choice B is correct.

Choice C: We have no values for any of the majors, so we cannot infer any relationships about the number of students in each major.

17. Correct answer: 117%

Choose values. Let the number of English majors in 2015 = 1,000. The number of biology majors in 2015 was thus 2,000. The number of Biology majors in 2017 was thus (2,000)(0.88)(1.08) = 1,900.8. The number of English majors in 2017 was (1,000)(0.97)(0.9) = 873. Now, use the percent greater formula: % greater = % of – 100%. Plug in the numbers: (1,900.8/873) × 100 – 100% = 117%.

18. Correct answer: 2/3

Plug in numbers: Let 1,200 = population of State X and 600 = population of State Y. Let the population concentration of State X = 12, and the population concentration of State Y = 4. Area is therefore population of state divided by population concentration. The ratio of the area of State X to the area of State Y is thus 100/150 =2/3.

19. Correct answer: 4

Plug in numbers. Let the original side length of the square = 3. In this case, the original area is 9. If the length of each side is doubled, then the length of each side is 6 and the corresponding area is 6^2 = 36. 36/9 = 4

20. Correct answer: 332642487

If 321,000,000 cubic miles is 96.5 %. Then we must find 1% by doing 321,000,000 / 96.5. This is 3326422.87. Then to find out what 100% is (which would be the total water on earth in cubic miles) we must multiply this by 100 to get 332642487.

Section 4: SAT Math Calculator

1. Correct answer: D

The purpose of this question is to understand the process of using geometry to find degree values of angles. Since l and m are parallel lines, the respective angles on both lines will have equivalent degree values. This means that a and w, b and x, and so on will be the same degree amount. A straight line is 180 degrees, so you know that angle d is 180−67=113 degrees; and therefore angle z, which has the same value, is also 113 degrees.

2. Correct answer: B

Let's begin by observing the larger angle. ∠ABC is cut into two 10-degree angles by BD−→−. This means that angles ∠ABD and ∠CBD equal 10 degrees. Next, we are told that BE−→ bisects ∠CBD, which creates two 5-degree angles. ∠ABE consists of ∠ABD, which is 10 degrees, and ∠DBE, which is 5 degrees. We need to add the two angles together to solve the problem.

∠ABE=∠ABD+∠DBE

∠ABE=10°+5°

∠ABE=15°

3. Correct answer: B

The perimeter of the pentagonal track is one third of a mile; one mile is equal to 5,280 feet, so the perimeter is

13 × 5,280=1,760 feet.

Each side of the pentagon has length one fifth of its perimeter, or

15 × 1,760=352 feet.

Jessica runs three and one half sides, or

312 × 352=1,232 feet.

This makes 1,200 feet the closest, and correct, choice.

4. Correct answer: D

Benny runs at a rate of eight miles an hour for ten minutes, or 1060=16 hours. The distance he runs is equal to his rate multiplied by his time, so, setting =8, t=16 in this formula:

d=rt

d=8 × 16=43 miles.

One mile comprises 5,280 feet, so this is equal to

43 × 5,280=7,040 feet.

Since each side of the track measures 264 feet, this means that Benny runs

7,040÷264=2623 side lengths.

This means Benny runs around the track for 25 side lengths, which is 5 complete times, back to Point A; he then runs one more complete side length to Point B; and, finally, he runs 23 of a side length, finishing closest to Point C.

5. Correct answer: A

Let x equal the measure of angle DPB. Because the measure of angle APC is eighty-one degrees larger than the measure of DPB, we can represent this angle's measure as x + 81. Also, because the measure of angle CPD is equal to the measure of angle DPB, we can represent the measure of CPD as x.

Since APB is a straight line, the sum of the measures of angles DPB, APC, and CPD must all equal 180; therefore, we can write the following equation to find x:

x + (x + 81) + x = 180

Simplify by collecting the x terms.

3x + 81 = 180

Subtract 81 from both sides.

3x = 99

Divide by 3.

x = 33.

This means that the measures of angles DPB and CPD are both equal to 33 degrees. The original question asks us to find the measure of angle CPB, which is equal to the sum of the measures of angles DPB and CPD.

measure of CPB = 33 + 33 = 66.

The answer is 66.

6.   Correct answer: D

Let x equal the measure of angle ABC, let y equal the measure of the supplement of angle ABC, and let z equal the measure of the complement of angle ABC.

Because x and y are supplements, the sum of their measures must equal 180. In other words, x + y = 180.

We are told that one-half of the measure of the supplement is equal to twice the measure of ABC. We could write this equation as follows:

(1/2) y = 2x.

Because x + y = 180, we can solve for y in terms of x by subtracting x from both sides. In other words, y = 180 − x. Next, we can substitute this value into the equation (1/2) y = 2x and then solve for x.

(1/2) (180-x) = 2x.

Multiply both sides by 2 to get rid of the fraction.

(180 − x) = 4x.

Add x to both sides.

180 = 5x.

Divide both sides by 5.

x = 36.

The measure of angle ABC is 36 degrees. However, the original question asks us to find the measure of the complement of ABC, which we denoted previously as z. Because the sum of the measure of an angle and the measure of its complement equals 90, we can write the following equation:

x + z = 90.

Now, we can substitute 36 as the value of x and then solve for z.

36 + z = 90.

Subtract 36 from both sides.

z = 54.

The answer is 54.

7. **Correct answer: D**

Refer to the following diagram while reading the explanation:

We know that angle b has to be equal to its vertical angle (the angle directly "across" the intersection). Therefore, it is 20°.

Furthermore, given the properties of parallel lines, we know that the supplementary angle to a must be 40°. Based on the rule for supplements, we know that a + 40° = 180°. Solving for a, we get a = 140°.

Therefore, a + b = 140° + 20° = 160°

8. **Correct answer: C**

Intersecting lines create two pairs of vertical angles which are congruent. Therefore, we can deduce that y = measure of angle AED.

Furthermore, intersecting lines create adjacent angles that are supplementary (sum to 180 degrees). Therefore, we can deduce that x + y + z + (measure of angle AED) = 360.

Substituting the first equation into the second equation, we get

x + (measure of angle AED) + z + (measure of angle AED) = 360

2(measure of angle AED) + x + z = 360

2(measure of angle AED) = 360 − (x + z)

Divide by two and get:

measure of angle AED = 180 − 1/2(x + z).

9. Correct answer: D

The answer to this problem is 12. This can be drawn as shown below (intersections marked in red).

We can also be sure that this is the maximal case because it is the largest answer selection. Were it not given as a multiple choice question, however, we could still be sure this was the largest. This is because no line can intersect a circle in more than 2 points. Keeping this in mind, we look at the construction of our initial shape. The square has 4 lines, and then each diagonal is an additional 2. We have thus drawn in 6 lines. The maximum number of intersections is therefore going to be twice this, or 12.

10. Correct answer: A

By properties of parallel lines, A+B = 180°, B = 45°, C = A = 135°, so $2 \times |B-C| = 2 \times |45-135| = 180$.

11. Correct answer: D

Since we know opposite angles are equal, it follows that angle $\angle AFE = 10°$ and $\angle BGE = 50°$.

Imagine a parallel line passing through point E. The imaginary line would make opposite angles with $\angle AFE$ & $\angle BGE$, the sum of which would equal $\angle FEG$. Therefore, $\angle FEG = 60°$.

$\cos(60) = 0.5 = \frac{EG}{EF} \rightarrow EF = \frac{EG}{0.5} = 20$

12. Correct answer: C

When the measure of an angle is added to the measure of its supplement, the result is always 180 degrees. Put differently, two angles are said to be supplementary if the sum of their measures is 180 degrees. For example, two angles whose measures are 50 degrees and 130 degrees are supplementary, because the sum of 50 and 130 degrees is 180 degrees.

The answer is $(10x+140)°$.

13. Correct answer: D

When two parallel lines are intersected by another line, the sum of the measures of the interior angles on the same side of the line is 180°. Therefore, the sum of the angle that is labelled as 100° and angle y is 180°. As a result, angle y is 80°.

Another property of two parallel lines that are intersected by a third line is that the corresponding angles are congruent. So, the measurement of angle x is equal to the measurement of angle y, which is 80°.

14. Correct answer: D

Let A represent the measure, in degrees, of angle A. By definition, the sum of the measures of A and its complement is 90 degrees. We can write the following equation to determine an expression for the measure of the complement of angle A.

A + measure of complement of A = 90

Subtract A from both sides.

measure of complement of A = 90 − A

Similarly, because the sum of the measures of angle A and its supplement is 180 degrees, we can represent the measure of the supplement of A as 180 − A.

The problem states that the measure of the supplement of A is 40 degrees larger than twice the measure of the complement of A. We can write this as 2(90-A) + 40.

Next, we must set the two expressions 180 − A and 2(90 − A) + 40 equal to one another and solve for A:

180 − A = 2(90 − A) + 40

Distribute the 2:

180 - A = 180 − 2A + 40

Add 2A to both sides:

180 + A = 180 + 40

Subtract 180 from both sides:

A = 40

Therefore, the measure of angle A is 40 degrees.

The question asks us to find the sum of the measures of the supplement and complement of A. The measure of the supplement of A is 180 − A = 180 − 40 = 140 degrees. Similarly, the measure of the complement of A is 90 − 40 = 50 degrees.

The sum of these two is 140 + 50 = 190 degrees.

15. Correct answer: C

Solve for a by adding 2 to each side to get 8a = 24. Divide by 8 to find a = 3. Plug a = 3 into the second equation to find 4(3) − 1 = 12 − 1 = 11.

Alternatively, you could save yourself some time by noticing that 8a − 2 is 2(4a − 1). If 2(4a −1) = 22, divide by 2 to get 4a − 1 = 11.

16. Correct answer: A

Twenty percent of the sweaters in the store are white, so there are 200 × 0.2 = 40 white sweaters. There are 200 − 40 = 160 sweaters remaining. Of the remaining sweaters, 160 × 0.4 = 64 are brown. That means that 160 − 64 = 96 are blue. There are 96 − 40 = 56 more blue sweaters than white sweaters.

17. Correct answers: B and D

Use the Average Pie to find that Jill's mean of 3.75 for 8 evaluations gives her a current total of 3.75 × 8 = 30 points. Use the Average Pie to find that if she needs an average of 4.0 for 12 scores, she needs 4.0 × 12 = 48 total points. Jill still needs 48 − 30 = 18 points. Her four remaining scores must total 18 or greater. Only answers B. and D. have a total of at least 18.

18. Correct answer: A

Your best bet is to plug in values for all the angles, keeping in mind that those inside the triangle must add up to 180°, the ones along BC must add up to 180, the ones along CD must add up to 180°, and the ones at A must add up to 90°. Then add up the marked angles.

19. Correct answer: D

Use the Group formula: Total = Group1 + Group2 − Both + Neither. In this problem the total is 2,400. The question also states that 1,200 students (half of the total) take calculus, so that is

Group1; one-third of that group (400) take both calculus and English. Because every student takes calculus or English or both, the Neither group is zero. Solve for the number of students who take English by plugging these numbers into the group formula: 2400 = 1200 + Group2 − 400. The number of students who take English is 1,600, or choice D.

20. Correct answer: B

Plug in the answers starting with choice C. Eventually you find B is the correct option.

21. Correct answer: D

5x + 3 = 7x − 1

now collect like terms

3 + 1 = 7x − 5x

4 = 2x

4/2 = x

2 = x

22. Correct answer: C

5x + 2(x + 7) = 14x − 7

5x + 2x + 14 = 14x − 7

7x + 14 = 14x − 7

7x − 14x = -14 − 7

-7x = -21

x = 3

23. Correct answer: B

Find the answer by initially solving for t.

- 8 = 2t

t = - 4

24. Correct answer: C

$5(z + 1) = 3(z + 2) + 11.$ $z = ?$

$5z + 5 = 3z + 6 + 11$

$5z + 5 = 3z + 17$

$5z = 3z + 17 - 5$

$5z - 3z = 12$

$2z = 12$

$z = 6$

25. Correct answer: D

The price increased from $20 to $25 ($5) so the question is 5 is what percent of 20. Or, $5/20 = x/100$; $500/20 = 25\%$

26. Correct answer: C

The book drops by 5 Dollars. 5 Dollars as a percentage of the total of 25 dollars is $5/25 = 20$ percent.

27. Correct answer: D

The first time, Brian answered 150 questions correctly and the second time he answered 30% more correctly, so,

$150 + (30/100 \times 150)$; 30% of 150 = 45, or $(30 \times 150)/100$

so $150 + 45 = 195$

28. Correct answer: B

Let us call this number x:

This number is increased by 2: $x + 2$

Then, it is multiplied by 3: $3(x + 2)$

The result is 24: $3(x + 2) = 24$ ... Solving this linear equation, we obtain the value of the number:

x + 2 = 24 / 3

x + 2 = 8

x = 8 − 2

x = 6

29. Correct answer: B

My age: x

My brother is 3 years older than me: x + 3

My father is 3 less than 2 times my age: 2x − 3

My father's age divided by 5 is equal to my brother's age divided by 3: (2x − 3) / 5 = (x + 3) / 3

By cross multiplication:

5(x + 3) = 3(2x − 3)

5x + 15 = 6x − 9

x = 24

My father's age: 2.24 − 3= 48 − 3 = 45

30. Correct answer: C

There are two fractions containing x and the denominators are different. First, let us find a common denominator to simplify the expression. The least common multiplier of 4 and 7 is 28. Then,

7(x − 2) / 28 − 4(3x + 5) / 28 = − 3x 28 / 28 ... Since both sides are written on the denominator 28 now, we can eliminate them:

7(x − 2) − 4(3x + 5) = − 84

7x − 14 − 12x − 20 = − 84

− 5x = − 84 + 14 + 20

− 5x = − 50

x = 50/5

x = 10

31. Correct answer: 3/7

To find x:

1 / (1 + 1 / (1 − 1/x)) = 4

This means that (1 + 1 / (1 − 1/x)) is equal to 1/4. Then,

1 + 1 / (1 − 1/x) = 1/4

1 / (1 − 1/x) = 1/4 − 1

1 / (1 − 1/x) = − 3/4

This means that 1 − 1/x = − 4/3. Then,

1 − 1/x = − 4/3

1 + 4/3 = 1/x

1/x = 7/3

So, x = 3/7.

32. Correct answer: A = 22.5 and B = 67.5

If A and B are complementary,

A+B=90 .... Equation 1

The measure of angle B is three times the measure of angle A

B=3A..............Equation 2

Substituting the value of B from equation 2 in equation 1, we get

A+3A=90

4A=90 and hence A=22.5

Putting this value of A in either of the equations and solving for B, we get

B=67.5

Hence, A=22.5and B=67.5

33. Correct answer: 0.68

68% equals 0.68

34. Correct answer: 16

The difference between each value is 2,4,8, Blank.

If this pattern is followed and the blank space is 16, then the next value would be 32.

18 plus 16 is 34. And then you can confirm that 34 plus 32 (the logical next value for the difference, does in fact equal 66).

35. Correct answer: 5287

36. Correct answer: 10

$3(x-4) = 18$

Divide by 3 to get

$x-4=6$

then add 4 to find:

$x=10$

37. Correct answer: 7 cm

Let A1 be the area of the trapezoid AEFD. Hence

$A1 = (1/2) h (AE + DF) = (1/2) h (3 + DF)$, h is the height of the parallelogram.

Now let A2 be the area of the trapezoid EBCF. Hence

$A2 = (1/2) h (EB + FC)$

We also have

$EB = 10 - AE = 7, FC = 10 - DF$

We now substitute EB and FC in $A2 = (1/2) h (EB + FC)$

A2 = (1/2) h (7 + 10 - DF) = (1/2) h (17 - DF)

For EF to divide the parallelogram into two regions of equal ares, we need to have area A1 and area A2 equal

(1/2) h (3 + DF) = (1/2) h (17 - DF)

Multiply both sides by 2 and divide thm by h to simplify to

3 + DF = 17 - DF

Solve for DF

2DF = 17 - 3

2DF = 14

DF = 7 cm

38. Correct answer: 87°

A first interior angle of the triangle is supplementary to the angle whose measure is 125° and is equal to

180 - 125 = 55°

A second interior angle of the triangle is supplementary to the angle whose measure is 142° and is equal to

180 - 142 = 38°

The sum of all three angles of the triangle is equal to 180°. Hence

A + 55 + 38 = 180

A = 180 - 55 - 38 = 87°

Section 5: SAT Essay Prompt

It's not easy to grade your own essay, but this rubric will help you to do so.

Score	Reading
1	The response demonstrates little or no comprehension of the source text. The response fails to show an understanding of the text's central idea(s), and may include only details without reference to central idea(s). The response may contain numerous errors of fact and/or interpretation with regard to the text. The response makes little or no use of textual evidence (quotations, paraphrases, or both), demonstrating little or no understanding of the source text.
2	The response demonstrates some comprehension of the source text. The response shows an understanding of the text's central idea(s) but not of important details. The response may contain errors of fact and/or interpretation with regard to the text. The response makes limited and/or haphazard use of textual evidence (quotations, paraphrases, or both), demonstrating some understanding of the source text.

3	The response demonstrates effective comprehension of the source text.
	The response shows an understanding of the text's central idea(s) and important details.
	The response is free of substantive errors of fact and interpretation with regard to the text.
	The response makes appropriate use of textual evidence (quotations, paraphrases, or both), demonstrating an understanding of the source text.
4	The response demonstrates thorough comprehension of the source text.
	The response shows an understanding of the text's central idea(s) and of most important details and how they interrelate, demonstrating a comprehensive understanding of the text.
	The response is free of errors of fact or interpretation with regard to the text.
	The response makes skillful use of textual evidence (quotations, paraphrases, or both), demonstrating a complete understanding of the source text.

Score	Analysis
1	The response offers little or no analysis or ineffective analysis of the source text and demonstrates little or no understanding of the analytic task.
	The response identifies without explanation some aspects of the author's use of evidence, reasoning, and/or stylistic and persuasive elements, and/or feature(s) of the student's choosing,
	Or numerous aspects of the response's analysis are unwarranted based on the text.
	The response contains little or no support for claim(s) or point(s) made, or support is largely irrelevant.
	The response may not focus on features of the text that are relevant to addressing the task,
	Or the response offers no discernible analysis (e.g., is largely or exclusively summary).
2	The response offers limited analysis of the source text and demonstrates only partial understanding of the analytical task.
	The response identifies and attempts to describe the author's use of evidence, reasoning, and/or stylistic and persuasive elements, and/or feature(s) of the student's own choosing, but merely asserts rather than explains their importance, or one or

	more aspects of the response's analysis are unwarranted based on the text.
	The response contains little or no support for claim(s) or point(s) made.
	The response may lack a clear focus on those features of the text that are most relevant to addressing the task.
3	The response offers an effective analysis of the source text and demonstrates an understanding of the analytical task.
	The response competently evaluates the author's use of evidence, reasoning, and/or stylistic and persuasive elements, and/or feature(s) of the student's own choosing.
	The response contains relevant and sufficient support for claim(s) or point(s) made.
	The response focuses primarily on those features of the text that are most relevant to addressing the task.
4	The response offers an insightful analysis of the source text and demonstrates a sophisticated understanding of the analytical task.
	The response offers a thorough, well-considered evaluation of the author's use of evidence, reasoning, and/or stylistic and persuasive elements, and/or feature(s) of the student's own choosing.

| | The response contains relevant, sufficient, and strategically chosen support for claim(s) or point(s) made. |
| | The response focuses consistently on those features of the text that are most relevant to addressing the task. |

Score	Writing
1	The response demonstrates little or no cohesion and inadequate skill in the use and control of language.
	The response may lack a clear central claim or controlling idea.
	The response lacks a recognizable introduction and conclusion. The response does not have a discernible progression of ideas.
	The response lacks variety in sentence structures; sentence structures may be repetitive. The response demonstrates general and vague word choice; word choice may be poor or inaccurate. The response may lack a formal style and objective tone.
	The response shows a weak control of the conventions of standard written English and may contain numerous errors that undermine the quality of writing.
2	The response demonstrates little or no cohesion and limited skill in the use and control of language.

	The response may lack a clear central claim or controlling idea or may deviate from the claim or idea over the course of the response.

The response may include an ineffective introduction and/or conclusion. The response may demonstrate some progression of ideas within paragraphs but not throughout the response.

The response has limited variety in sentence structures; sentence structures may be repetitive.

The response demonstrates general or vague word choice; word choice may be repetitive. The response may deviate noticeably from a formal style and objective tone. |
| 3 | The response is mostly cohesive and demonstrates effective use and control of language.

The response includes a central claim or implicit controlling idea.

The response includes an effective introduction and conclusion. The response demonstrates a clear progression of ideas both within paragraphs and throughout the essay.

The response has variety in sentence structures. The response demonstrates |

	some precise word choice. The response maintains a formal style and objective tone. The response shows a good control of the conventions of standard written English and is free of significant errors that detract from the quality of writing.
4	The response is cohesive and demonstrates a highly effective use and command of language. The response includes a precise central claim. The response includes a skillful introduction and conclusion. The response demonstrates a deliberate and highly effective progression of ideas both within paragraphs and throughout the essay. The response has a wide variety in sentence structures. The response demonstrates a consistent use of precise word choice. The response maintains a formal style and objective tone. The response shows a strong command of the conventions of standard written English and is free or virtually free of errors.

Scoring Guide

On each section of the SAT , the number of correct answers converts to a scaled score of 1–36. SAT will adjust the scaling for each exam so that each set of results are fair and representative of performance. No one SAT test date is "easier" than the others, but there will be variations in scoring. This is standard practice with standardized testing.

Calculate Your SAT Score

SAT Raw Score vs Scale Score

You will score one mark for each of the total number of questions you get right on each test (English, Math, Reading, and Science) equals your raw score. Your raw score for each test is then converted into a scale score.

Composite Score

Your composite score, or overall SAT score, is the average of your scores on each test. Add up your English, Math, Reading, and Science scores and divide by 4. (Round to the nearest whole number).

Sample SAT Scoring Chart

Overview

The SAT is scored out of 1600 in the end. This is a scaled score and you will need to convert your raw score (what you have actually scored) into this value.

The two main sections are Evidence-Based Reading and Writing (EBRW), and Math. You can earn a scaled score of between 200 and 800 points on each section, for a total of 1600 possible points on the SAT.

Raw scores become scaled through a process that College Board calls equating. Equating makes sure that the different forms of the test or the level of ability of the students with whom you are tested do not affect your score. This therefore means that it is possible to make comparisons among test takers who take different editions of the test across different administrations.

This therefore means that rather than being compared against only the people who sit the test on the day that you sit it, it also allows for variations in the difficulties in past tests. This means that a 700 on SAT Math in the Spring has to represent the same ability level as a 700 on SAT Math in Summer. So if the Summer test turns out to be more difficult for students, the raw-score to scaled-score calculation will be adjusted so that a slightly lower raw points total still achieves a 700 scaled score.

Since the equating formula changes from test to test to keep the scores equal, there is no way to know for sure how a certain raw score will translate to a scaled score. However, the College Board releases raw score to scaled score ranges to give you an idea of what level of raw score you need to get to certain scaled score numbers.

Raw Score Conversion Table			
Raw Score	Math Section Score	Reading Test Score	Writing and Language Score
0	200	10	10
1	200	10	10
2	210	10	10
3	230	11	10
4	240	12	11
5	260	13	12
6	280	14	13
7	290	15	13
8	310	15	14

Raw Score Conversion Table			
Raw Score	Math Section Score	Reading Test Score	Writing and Language Score
9	320	16	15
10	330	17	16
11	340	17	16
12	360	18	17
13	370	19	18
14	380	19	19
15	390	20	19
16	410	20	20
17	420	21	21

Raw Score Conversion Table			
Raw Score	Math Score Section	Reading Test Score	Writing/ Language Score
18	430	21	21
19	440	22	22
20	450	22	23
21	460	23	23
22	470	23	24
23	480	24	25
24	480	24	25
25	490	25	26
26	500	25	26
27	510	26	27
28	520	26	28
29	520	27	28
30	530	28	29
31	540	28	30
32	550	29	30
33	560	30	31
34	560	30	32
35	570	31	32
36	580	31	33
37	590	32	34
38	600	32	34

Raw Score Conversion Table			
Raw Score	Math Score Section	Reading Test Score	Writing/ Language Score
39	600	32	35
40	610	33	36
41	620	33	37
42	630	34	38
43	640	35	39
44	650	35	40
45	660	36	
46	670	37	
47	670	37	
48	680	38	
49	690	38	
50	700	39	
51	710	40	
52	730	40	
53	740		
54	750		
55	760		
56	780		
57	790		
58	800		

Calculating Your Math Section Score

Finding your score on SAT Math is simple.

1. Find out your raw score on each of the two math sections (No Calculator and Calculator). This is just the total amount of questions you answered correctly.

   The No Calculator section has 20 possible points, while the Calculator section has 38 possible points. Empty or incorrect questions do not count for or against you.

2. Add your No-Calculator raw score to your Calculator raw scorethe maximum available raw score is 58.

3. Using the table for your practice test, find the scaled score of 200-800 your raw score matches to.

Finding Your Reading and Writing Score

Finding your EBRW scaled score is a bit harder than for your Math score, since you have to combine your performance on the Reading and Writing sections

1. Find your raw score on the Reading section. This is just the total amount of questions you answered correctly. Blank or wrong questions do not count for or against you. The highest raw score possible is 52.

2. Find your raw score on the Writing section. This is just the total amount of questions you answered correctly. Blank or wrong questions do not count for or against you. The highest raw score possible is 44.

3. Find your Reading "scaled score" on the table. This is a number between 10 and 40.

4. Find your Writing "scaled score" on the table. This is a number between 10 and 40.

5. Add your Reading and Writing scaled scores together.

6. Multiply your scaled score by 10. This is your final scaled score between 200 and 800.

Now, calculate your total SAT composite score, since you know you Math score and your EBRW score. Now add them together to get the composite.

Good Luck!

So that's it! You've done the practicetest, I hope it went well. I wish you the best of luck in your future endeavors and hope that you make it to the school that you want! Your job now is to keep practicing and preparing, use my advice for test preparation, and may I take this opportunity to wish you good luck!

Printed in Great Britain
by Amazon